Step Up and Lead

STEP UP

AND

LEAD

FRANK VISCUSO

Fire Engineering
BOOKS & VIDEOS

Copyright © 2013 by
Fire Engineering Books & Videos
110 S. Hartford Ave., Suite 200
Tulsa, Oklahoma 74120 USA
800.752.9764

+1.918.831.9421
info@fireengineeringbooks.com
www.FireEngineeringBooks.com

Marketing Manager: Amanda Alvarez
National Account Manager: Cindy J. Huse

Director: Mary McGee
Managing Editor: Marla Patterson
Production Manager: Sheila Brock
Production Editor: Tony Quinn
Book Designer: Susan E. Ormston
Cover Designer: Charles Thomas

Library of Congress Cataloging-in-Publication Data

Viscuso, Frank.
  Step up and lead / Frank Viscuso.
    pages cm
  Includes index.
  ISBN 978-1-59370-308-0
1. Leadership. 2. Customer service. I. Title.
HD57.7.V57 2013
658.4'092--dc23
                              2012047146

Printed in the United States of America

8 9 10 11   22 21 20

To my boys Nicholas, Frank Jr., and Thomas—
May God give you the strength to step up
when necessary, make good decisions,
and always do the right thing.

Contents

Foreword

Vincent Dunn, Deputy Chief (Ret.) FDNY and best-selling author

The most effective leadership principles I have learned have come from strong leaders within the fire service. Some fire officers are great at leading around the fire station. Others are born to lead on the fireground. Every so often you come across a fire officer leader in both environments. Deputy Chief Frank Viscuso is one of those leaders.

For years, Frank has been educating and motivating people at his seminars. His most popular teaching is based on the leadership and team-building skills that are featured in this book. Coming off the success of his best-selling book *Fireground Operational Guides*, Frank has established himself as one of the most credible and influential authors and educators within the fire service. In *Step Up and Lead*, he takes the same simple approach used in *Operational Guides* and provides readers with step-by-step strategy and tactics that can be used when setting goals, motivating teams, dealing with difficult people, communicating effectively, tackling administrative tasks, providing exceptional customer service, and much more. *Step Up* also introduces readers to thirteen essential traits a fire service leader should possess. In short, this book explains how to lead by creating your organization's culture by design, rather than default.

Strong leadership skills are essential for the survival of any profession. This is especially true in the fire service. There is a reason why people relate firefighters to words like courage, brotherhood, and respect. That reason is decades of great leadership. If you are looking to increase the effectiveness and productivity of you and your team, you have purchased the right book. *Step Up and Lead* reveals the leadership principles and skills that fire service leaders use to motivate and lead teams through some of the most adverse conditions and situations known. In this book, Frank draws from his personal experiences as a fire officer and provides proven techniques that will benefit anyone who is looking to lead a successful team.

This book does not belong on your bookshelf, it belongs on your desk, dog-eared, highlighted, and written in. Don't just read it. Use it. Regardless of whether you feel you are ready to lead, you are ready to receive the message in this important book.

Acknowledgments

To the team at PennWell, especially Cindy Huse, Janie Green, Tony Quinn, Amanda Alvarez, and Marla Patterson. You rock! Thank you for putting your confidence in me. I am proud to be a part of the best team in the business. To my friend and fellow cocreator of FireOpsOnline.com, Chris Stopero—you are often the first person I bounce ideas off and ask, "Is this any good?" Thanks for never holding back from telling me the truth.

To my brother Joe Viscuso and my pals Mike Terpak and Bryan Emenecker, you three are the best of the best—true leaders within the fire service. I learn from your examples every day. To the members of the Kearny Fire Department, I would match your talents, skills, and abilities against any other organization in the country. I truly appreciate Bobby Halton, PJ Norwood, Jim Duffy, Don Colarusso, and Ryan Chamberlin for the examples you set in your fields. You guys definitely understand what it means to *step up and lead!*

A special thank you goes to the amazingly talented Paul Combs. I am in awe of your ability to tell a complete story with your illustrations (some of which are featured in this book). Your work will forever be considered an important contribution to the fire service. I strongly encourage anyone who is reading this to pick up a copy of Paul's book *Drawn by Fire*. So many wonderful photographers have also contributed to this book, I want to thank them all, especially Brett Dzadik, Stephen Walsh, Cindy Rashkin, Constantine Sypsomos, the crew at newjerseyfireground.com, Ron Jeffers, and Andrew Taylor, Jr.

To my mother, father, and sisters Donna and Denise: The four of you have been there for me through all of life's highs and lows. I smile daily because you are my blood relatives. I laugh because there is nothing any of you can do about it.

I am blessed beyond words to have the most supportive wife imaginable. Whenever I feel pressure or stress that often accompanies the act of stepping out of my comfort zone, the one person who never doubts my ability is my beautiful wife Laura. Thank you for being an amazing wife and the most wonderful mother our boys could ever imagine. I love you!

A LEADER OF ONE

Who's In Charge?

In the fire service, every incident has an incident commander (IC). The IC is the person in charge of the overall operation. When a firefighter, or anyone else for that matter, arrives on scene, he or she can easily identify the IC. It might be the white helmet and the reflective vest, or perhaps it's the presence of a strategically placed command post. You can go anywhere in the country, and wherever you find a large-scale incident happening, there will always be identifiable characteristics that will help you determine who is in charge (fig. 1–1).

Leaders, on the other hand, are not always as easy to identify. They may look like everyone else in the room. They may not have a title (which is often confused with leadership). They may not even have a following—yet—but they are leaders.

All of us have an inherent need for a clear sense of direction and purpose in life. Everyone wants to be a part of something great. Sometimes, the only thing that is missing is someone to lead the way. That person can be you.

Fig. 1–1. The IC on the fireground is always easy to identify. Leaders, on the other hand, may look like everyone else in the room—it's their actions that set them apart.

The world is full of critics. It doesn't take much to be one. All you need is a mouth and an opinion. Such people are great at finding problems and bringing attention to those problems. They are also great at criticizing others. I believe that people who criticize often wish they were more like the people they are criticizing. And let's face it, since the beginning of time, the world has never erected a statue of a critic.

Leadership requires courage and determination. Leadership also requires action. To lead, you will have to step away from the pack because that is usually where the problem lies. You will find that little minds travel in groups. Until, that is, someone decides to *step up and lead* those groups to a better place.

No One Trained Me!

If I had a dollar for every time someone said, "No one told me that," or, "How was I supposed to know?" I'd have a house in the Hamptons.

In case you haven't realized it yet, most of the time these excuses are made, people see right through them. The fact is, the fire service may have been blessed with great leaders, but make no mistake about it, we've had our share of ineffective ones as well. When a person attains a high-ranking position in the fire service, that individual may hold that position for a long time. Ineffective leaders usually do little or nothing to train their successors. In an organization that has no leadership/officer development or mentorship program, this can create a serious problem. When people in positions of leadership make mistakes, they will simply throw their hands up and cry, "No one trained me!"

It doesn't matter if an organization promotes people based on a testing procedure or strictly on achievement, success, and merit. Individuals are sometimes promoted beyond their level of ability. This is called the Peter Principle. The principle is commonly phrased, "Employees tend to rise to their level of incompetence." In more formal jargon, the effect could be stated as this: Employees tend to be given more authority until they cannot continue to work competently. This theory was formulated by Dr. Laurence J. Peter and Raymond Hull in their 1969 book *The Peter Principle*. When this scenario occurs, the go-to excuse most people fall back on is, "It's not my fault. No one trained me to do this!"

This excuse promotes a culture of complacency. Complacency is unacceptable on the fireground. Here's an example to illustrate why: When responding to a fire call in a high-rise apartment complex, two firefighters (a captain and a senior firefighter) met the building super-intendent in the lobby. The dispatcher called the firefighters over the radio to inform them that the original caller called back and said it was nothing more than a pot on the stove. Traditionally, these types of incidents cause a lot of smoke, but no real heat or fire threat, especially when they are discovered early and the stove is shut off, which was exactly what the firefighters were told happened. The two firefighters jumped on the elevator and rode it up to the 11th floor, where the incident was. The department's procedure at high-rise fires is to take the elevator two stories below the fire then take the stairs to the fire floor; however, there was no need for that here. They had already received confirmation there was no problem.

In the elevator, the captain was sharing a funny story about something that happened to him the past weekend. They were both laughing when the elevator doors opened. It took less than two full seconds for the intense heat and flames to force them down to the bottom of the elevator car. Quickly placing their masks on, the two firefighters, who didn't have any tools with them, hastily made their way to the stairwell so they could get back to a safe place and call for help. They survived, but the lesson was learned: in our profession, complacency can kill.

"It's not my fault. No one trained me!" That may be true in your case. Maybe your organization didn't do a good job of providing you with the tools you need to be proficient at your job; but there is good news. Are you ready? Here it is . . . *you* can change that. Your first step is to realize that you are using this excuse. I admit it, I used this excuse in the past, so don't be too hard on yourself. The second step is to take corrective actions. Then, stop making excuses and start making progress. There is no shortage of information out there to help you grow and improve in your ability to lead (fig. 1–2). You don't have to wait for someone else to take charge. You can be the one to step up!

Fig. 1–2. There is no shortage of information available for you to begin your journey of becoming a better leader in your field.

Permission To Lead

No one anoints a leader. A person may be promoted to a position or a rank, but no one assigns a leader. Leadership is movement, not position. Leadership is a choice, but so is procrastination.

You don't have to ask for permission to be a leader. That doesn't mean you should begin by taking on the responsibility of your entire organization (although that may be your calling), it simply means that you have decided to begin leading *you*. One of my favorite sayings is, "A leader of one can one day be a leader of many, but if you can't lead one, you'll never lead any." That quote has always made me think about the importance of taking ownership of myself. You may be thinking, ownership of me? What does that mean? It simply means that you have taken the first step toward realizing your own full potential.

....

"A leader of one can one day be a leader of many,

but if you can't lead one, you'll never lead any."

....

We are all human beings with the same basic needs. We want to feel loved. We want to provide for those we love. We want to matter and make a difference somehow, some way. For many, the most fulfilling way to make a difference is to lead others in a mission of some sort. But to do so, we must first learn to lead ourselves. If you can't lead *you*, you can't lead, *period*.

You may think you are not the right person for the job. Have you ever stopped to consider how ironic it is that the largest social network in the world—Facebook—was created by someone who is considered to be socially awkward, Mark Zuckerberg? Perhaps you have convinced yourself that you are too small and insignificant. If you think you are too small to have an impact, try going to bed with a mosquito in the room. You may think you are too new to your organization to lead. I believe the best time to lead is when you are the most passionate about a cause. It doesn't matter whether you have been with your organization for a week or 30 years.

Leadership is about taking charge and influencing others to follow your vision. If you think about it, the majority of the time, leadership requires that a person go in the opposite direction of the crowd, rather than simply following it (fig. 1–3). Turning your back on the crowd takes courage. Although this is not a natural instinct, it may be necessary in order for you to take charge. The word *courage* may be synonymous with the word *firefighter*, but that doesn't make the act of leading any less challenging for a member of the fire service.

Fig. 1–3. Firefighters are used to going in the opposite direction of the crowd. The same principle often applies to leadership—look which way the crowd is going and go the other way.

Leaders in the Fire Service

Firefighters are a special breed. Any person who is willing to run into a burning building, even as a follower, is still exhibiting an essential leadership quality—the ability to put the needs of others ahead of one's own (fig. 1–4).

Fig. 1–4. A person who is willing to run into a burning building is clearly willing to put the needs of others first.

I have been blessed to be able to spend more than 20 years in the fire service. In that time, I have been around some of the strongest and most effective leaders in the world. To be a leader in the fire service industry is something special. There's not much room for error. Kurt Russell's character in the movie *Backdraft* said, "If you have a bad day here, somebody dies." Have you ever wondered how to create the type of loyalty that is found in the fire service? What does it take to get another human being to willingly risk his or her life while carrying out an order from another human being? We see it in the military. But often-times, these are young boys and girls fresh out of high school. In the fire service, we are dealing with grown men and women who have had many years of experiences that have shaped their opinions and character (for better or worse). We aren't always dealing with a clean slate. Regardless of age, race, religion, and past experiences, strong leaders will be able to motivate those around them.

Strong leadership is absolutely essential for the survival of any profession. This is especially true in the fire service. Corporate America would love to emulate two things that are deeply instilled in the fire service—the *brotherhood* and the *respect* of the public (fig. 1–5). There is a reason people relate our profession to words like *courage*, *brotherhood*, and *respect*. That reason is decades of great leadership.

Fig. 1–5. Corporate America would love to emulate two distinguishing characteristics that the fire service has become known for—brotherhood and respect from the public.

There may be a tradition of excellence within the fire service, but as with the rest of America, major changes have occurred in our profession since 9/11. Many organizations today are facing challenges that include downsizing, enormous competitive demands, extraordinary pressure, rapidly advancing technology, financial constraints, and staying in business. Make no mistake about it, those are the same challenges we are all facing in the fire service. For years, firefighters have been presented with the challenge of having to do more with less. I remember signing up to fight fires. In the blink of an eye, we became a key component in the first line of defense against terrorism in our country. That's quite a change in job description. One day we were conducting a drill on hoseline advancement, the next day we were setting up mass-casualty decontamination showers.

Like a working fire, the fire service is never stagnant or content (fig. 1–6). We are constantly changing and adapting—sometimes not by choice. In recent years, economic challenges have forced cutbacks, staffing reductions, and in some cases the demotion of or elimination of management and supervisory positions. As a result of politically motivated attacks on the pension system and benefit packages that have been promised to career firefighters, many have left the fire service years before they planned to retire in an effort to preserve what they had worked for. This has caused a problem that many organizations have not seen before. We are losing seasoned, knowledgeable firefighters through rapid turnover rates. As a result, firefighters have been quickly moving through the ranks, many without having a chance to develop leadership qualities. Because of this, *Step Up and Lead* was written to serve two purposes:

- To introduce firefighters to the essential traits and skills that every effective fire service leader should possess

- To teach those outside of the fire service the secrets of effective leadership from one of the most respected organizations in the world

In difficult and challenging times, it's essential that new leaders step up. Whether it's the years of experience and knowledge that are leaving the fire service at a record rate or the lack of funding that most municipalities are dealing with (which doesn't allow for fire departments to retain numbers or maintain and update necessary equipment), the fire service has its fair share of challenges.

Fig. 1–6. Like a working fire, the fire service is never stagnant or content. We are constantly changing and adapting—sometimes not by choice.

Our industry's distinct identity can be both good and bad. It's good because we have a tradition of bravery and excellence that we continue to build on—a tradition that has been respected, honored, and cherished throughout the years by many strong leaders. On the other hand, it's bad because every time a firefighter does something wrong, it affects the entire industry. Any time you read about an isolated event, it gives our profession a black eye. It doesn't matter what the incident is, any incident involving a firefighter doing something wrong affects the entire fire service in the public's eyes. For example, the news won't just report that John Doe was arrested for allegedly doing xyz. Instead, it will say, "Firefighter John Doe . . ."

There are bad teachers, doctors, lawyers, and airline pilots in the world. There are also bad firefighters. When someone who works for an organization like yours makes a poor decision, it's easy to blame the individual. After all, we are all responsible for our own actions. But the cold hard truth is that sometimes at the heart of these problems are the leaders. Perhaps your organization is suffering from a disconnect between the leaders and the rank and file. If so, it's time for a change. It's time to restore hope, values, and discipline. This only begins when you first discipline yourself. Remember, if you can't lead one, you'll never lead any.

I need to stress the point that a person doesn't need to be an officer or a manager to be a leader. On the contrary, leaders are often apparent before they earn a title. I believe I am speaking for the majority of chief officers in the fire service when I say one of the most valuable assets on the fireground is a firefighter who thinks like a leader (fig. 1–7).

Fig. 1–7. When carrying out assignments on the fireground, firefighters who think like leaders will make quality decisions.

The same can be said for those who display leadership qualities around the fire station and when dealing with the public. I have had the good fortune of working with and learning from several firefighters who fit into this category. Throughout this book I will introduce some of them to you.

One of them is Chris Stopero. When he first came on the job, Chris would admit that he did not display the qualities of a leader. One of the guys on the shift he was assigned to enjoyed spending most of his downtime in the recliner. He would misguide Chris by saying things like, "Chris, get some rest. Fatigue is a firefighter's worst enemy."

Chris, trying to fit in, thought the right thing to do was to take the seat next to him, even though it went against his ambitious nature. One day, Chris was working with a captain who wasn't normally assigned to his shift. After an incident, Chris sat in the recliner. The captain walked up to him and said, "What are you doing?" Chris replied, with, "You know, Cap. Fatigue is a firefighter's worst enemy."

The captain flipped. He could not comprehend how a guy with fewer than three months on the job would have the gall to say such a thing. After the captain reprimanded Chris, things changed quickly. Today, I can tell you with absolute certainty that Chris is one of the most effective leaders I have ever had the honor of working with. He's not only a great firefighter, but a great communicator who brings many fresh ideas and skills to the table. Chris and I partnered up to develop FireOpsOnline.com, a website that offers free fire training, drills, and tips for career and volunteer firefighters. Although he started on the wrong foot, he credits that captain—Jerry Coppola—for putting him in his place and saying the words he needed to hear.

It's Not About You!

Although it begins with you, it's not all about you. One quality that serves leaders well is humility. You may lead the greatest team in the world, but remember that the key word in that phrase is *team* (fig. 1–8). When things go right, do you take the credit? Be careful before you answer. Taking credit for the results of a team is a two-way street. If you are going to take credit when things go well, you have to take the blame when things don't go well.

The success of an organization depends very much on a leader's ability to inspire. Although there are many other aspects, one individual's attitude and ability to motivate others can make or break an entire organization. Failure to inspire others will result in organizational failure. Most people who read that last sentence immediately begin to point fingers at their superior and say, "You see, he is the reason why things are so messed up around here!" or "If she understood how bad a leader she is, we might be able to fix this problem." Well, I have news for them. The success of an organization is not solely the responsibility of *one* person. The success of an organization, however, absolutely is a result of one person's ability to motivate others to take action. That person can be *you*.

Fig. 1–8. A group of firefighters working together is a perfect example of teamwork.

Most people are creatures of habit. Unfortunately, our habits aren't always good ones. It's very easy to fall into what I call the coma of complacency. This primarily happens because we are drawn to familiarity. Some call this a *comfort zone*. My first recollection of making a poor decision based on familiarity was when I visited the University of Charleston in West Virginia for the first time. I had chosen to attend the university because I was offered a crew scholarship, and they had a strong art program. Yes, I know, it's crazy. I wanted to be an artist, but ended up becoming a firefighter. I am truly grateful things worked out the way they did.

When I arrived on campus, I was brought to my dorm where I was given the choice of which side I wanted to live on. One side had a view of a beautiful courtyard with a vibrant garden. The other overlooked a very busy (and loud) road with railroad tracks across the street. A train was passing by at the time. It was a freight train, about half a mile long and moving super slowly. I quickly chose that side. Why? Because back home, I lived three houses away from a very busy road and two houses away from railroad tracks. I chose familiarity. I chose to remain in my comfort zone.

How many of us have made similar decisions in our lives? How many times have you chosen to do the thing that you were familiar with because you were reluctant to step away from what you already knew? What I didn't realize at the time was that no one ever finds success in his or her comfort zone. On that note, I can also tell you that you cannot successfully lead an organization while sitting on your couch. The only way to lead is to take action and step outside of your comfort zone (fig. 1–9).

Fig. 1–9. There are no comfort zones on the fireground. In order to be successful, a leader will have to step into unfamiliar territory.

The Mission

On September 17, 2011, a protest called Occupy Wall Street was organized in Zuccotti Park, located in New York City's Wall Street financial district. The protest was initiated by a Canadian activist group. It was the first of many Occupy protests that sprang up throughout the world. Their initial purpose was to take a stand against corporate greed, economic inequality, and undue influence of financial services corporations on government. Their slogan, "We are the 99%," was in reference to the growing income inequality and wealth distribution in the United States between the wealthiest 1% and the rest of the population.

For months, every time you turned on the news, someone was talking about Occupy Wall Street and its spinoff protests. Sounds like it was a success, right? It wasn't. The reason it failed was because they didn't have a leader. Every time someone was interviewed, the person was trying to bring light to a different issue. One person was talking about corporate greed, another was talking about racial inequality, and another was talking about gay rights. It seemed like anybody who was fed up with anything showed up and said whatever was on his or her mind. There was no unified message, no clarity of purpose, no obvious leader, just a group of people in tents taking a stand against . . . well, that all depends on who you asked. The only reason I know when it started, where it started, and by whom is because I Googled it.

I am not trying to minimize any individual's reason for participating. I actually agree with some of what they stood for; I am only providing an example to illustrate the point that just getting people to show up isn't leadership. You need a clearly defined mission. If you have ever heard me speak, you will often hear me use the word *clarity*. As a leader, it is important that others know what you stand for and what you expect to accomplish. There is a simple reason this is so important: Clarity promotes unity. Confusion creates stagnation.

....

"A group of people marching without a mission are just taking a walk."

....

What is your mission? Are you interested in showing the upper management of your organization that you are an up-and-comer? Are you interested in taking a group of disgruntled workers and getting them excited again? Are you looking to develop and lead a team that wins . . . every time? It doesn't matter what decisions you have made in the past. The past is the past. Your rearview mirror is smaller than your front windshield for a reason. You may be the newest member of your organization, but you are interested in earning a promotion. If you think you can do it, you can. When I was a probationary firefighter, I used to clean the deputy chief's office every morning. Although some people may find it demoralizing cleaning toilets, mopping the floor, and emptying the wastebasket, I used the few moments I spent in that office to visualize myself becoming a chief officer one day. After all, someone had to step up, why not me? Why not you (fig. 1–10)?

Fig. 1–10. Someone is going to step up and be promoted to the position you want. Why not you?

Nothing is forever. Like most organizations, the fire service is changing every day. You may or may not realize it, and it may or may not be for the better, but your industry is changing. Life's too short to fight the forces of change. Life's also too short to hate what you do all day. Make it your mission to create the positive change you want to see.

Perhaps your current leadership doesn't seem to realize things are crumbling around it. You may have proposed a great idea only to have it fall upon deaf ears. Poor leaders do not always agree with good ideas. Why? Because they are poor leaders.

A New Generation of Leaders

Society in general is in need of a new generation of leaders. This becomes evident every time there is an important political election and most of us turn to others and say, "Are these people really our best options?" The same sentiments may be predominant within your organization. Unfortunately, this is common, which is why we are in need of a new generation of leaders.

Leadership requires vision. A leader's job is to look into the future and see his or her organization, not as it is, but as it will be. Leadership—and I mean true leadership—also requires well-developed people skills. Most firefighters can think back to the early days of their career and remember an officer or senior member of their organization who inspired them to be better. It's not uncommon to hear that these people did not only help make others become better firefighters, but they also impacted lives. What made those firefighters so effective? What traits did they possess? How did they handle difficult people or situations? Those questions will be answered in the next few chapters.

....

"A leader's job is to look into the future

and see his or her organization,

not as it is, but as it will be."

....

I remember being invited to my friend and fellow firefighter Terrence Byrnes's father's retirement party. Terry's father, James Byrnes, was a well-respected fire chief from Jersey City—one of the busiest departments in the state. Chief Byrnes had a reputation for being knowledgeable and strong in his convictions. I had never worked with him, but I heard he was "tough to work for because he demanded a lot from people." This is not a bad quality if you go about it the right way. Until his retirement party, I had no idea whether he did this, but the answer became evident on that night. His retirement party began like any other one—great food, music, and stories. Then came the moment when a group of firefighters who worked with Chief Byrnes went to the front of the room to say a few words about him. Within a few minutes, there was not a dry eye in the room, including the firefighters in front. I know what you're thinking—firefighters don't cry. This may be true, but their eyeballs sometimes sweat. The truth is some of the most emotional and passionate people I have ever met were firefighters. These guys were no different. They loved their leader. I remember thinking on that day that if I end my career with people feeling the same way about me, I will have succeeded as a fire service leader.

I have often thought back and contemplated what made Chief Byrnes a great fire chief. Yes, he was knowledgeable, and yes, he loved his job. Both are essential traits. He also demanded more from everyone, which is usually something that people don't value until a leader is gone. But there was something else he had that many people in leadership positions seem to be missing—great relationships with the people he was leading. Relationships keep teams together. We will discuss more about relationships throughout this book. It was also obvious, from the stories that were told that night, that Chief Byrnes was respected because he made good decisions, which is another topic we will cover thoroughly in chapters 2, 3, and 4.

You won't become a leader because you made one good decision. Leadership is constant. Your level of responsibility will increase with every advancement or promotion (fig. 1–11). Your thinking should increase and evolve as well. This doesn't mean you will never make mistakes. It simply means you should always look to improve. When I became a tour commander, I met with all the members of my group to share my thoughts with them. One of the things I told them was, "My number one job is to make sure you go home at the end of your shift."

For me, that was forward thinking. After all, even though I assumed it was also the top priority of some of the tour commanders I worked for in the past, I wasn't 100% sure of it because none of them ever looked me in my eyes and said those exact words to me. I felt it was important that the members of my tour understood that I respected and cared enough about them to ensure them that I put their well-being above all else, which is why I call for a rehab unit early at fires. I also understood that they put the well-being of the citizens they are protecting ahead of their own. They deserved that same amount of respect in return (fig. 1–12).

Fig. 1–11. Responsibility comes with leadership. The higher your rank, the heavier the load.

Fig. 1–12. One of the jobs of a leader is to identify and take care of the people who are working hard. At a fire scene, this means ensuring that people take time to rest and rehab.

One day I was reading a message from Rick Lasky, a retired fire chief from the city of Lewisville, Texas, and author of the book *Pride and Ownership*. His message read:

> To all Firefighters:
>
> I used to say it's my job to make sure you go home at the end of the shift or call, but I'll never say that again! I think it's short-ranged. We need to start thinking long-range and about the future. Now I say it's my job to make sure you go home at the end of your career as a paid or volunteer firefighter, with two good knees, a good back, and cancer free. Enough with thinking just about tomorrow! Let's invest in our people!

Immediately upon reading that message, I knew I had to revise my thinking, because it was, in fact, short-ranged. Chief Lasky is a great example of a leader. He is the type of person who makes others feel valued. It's impossible to leave his presence without feeling better about yourself and your potential. He is certainly helping to do his part in developing a new generation of leaders (fig. 1–13).

Fig. 1–13. Chief Lasky has made a positive impact on the fire service and my personal career.

Don't pass up the opportunity to be around people you believe are great leaders. You will never improve if you don't spend time around people who are doing things more effectively than you are. Your chances of achieving the success you desire will improve markedly when you surround yourself with people you want to be like rather than the people who want to be like you.

You also don't want to ignore the opportunity to lead when it is presented. Once you establish yourself as the type of person who steps up, you will begin to attract more opportunities. The alternative is to ignore your opportunity to lead and risk turning into someone who fights to protect the status quo at all costs, never asking if obedience is doing you (or your organization) any good. Bestselling author Seth Godin refers to this type of person as a "sleepwalker," and trust me, sleepwalkers don't do very well in this day and age.

Human beings have a deep-rooted desire to belong. We are attracted to groups of like-minded people. We are also attracted to leaders with vision, who are passionate about their cause. We live in a society that no longer expects leadership to come solely from the highest-ranking person in an organization. In the fire service, and now in corporate America, everyone in an organization—not just the boss—is expected to lead (fig. 1–14).

Fig. 1–14. Firefighters of all ranks have the responsibility to develop their leadership skills and increase their knowledge the way this group is by attending a weekend seminar.

Managers versus Leaders

There is a distinct difference between management and leadership. Managers manage a process they've seen before. Leaders create change. Although your thesaurus may say the best synonym for *leadership* is *management*, these are actually two very different concepts.

I can vividly remember sitting in my chief's office as a young officer as he added to my already heavy workload. I could not comprehend how he could possibly think I had enough time, energy, and talent to get so many projects completed in what felt like an unrealistic time frame.

One of the most common things I said during that time of my life was, "My brain is going to explode." Perhaps you can relate. Think back to an experience you have had in your life with an ineffective leader. Have you ever felt that you were expected to do more than others around you? Have you ever worked to improve yourself and your organization while others seemed disengaged without consequence? Have you ever felt overworked, underappreciated, and uninspired? If so, you may have worked under an ineffective leader. Learn from the experience. Sometimes we need to experience what doesn't work so that we can better understand what does. In unstable times, growth comes from leaders who create change and engage their organizations rather than managers who push their employees to do more for less.

Great leaders don't focus on trying to get people to do something. They focus on trying to get people to *be* something. Imagine how much more productive you would be if your boss or a teammate were constantly helping you become more than you thought you could be. This is a stark contrast to the way most "bosses" operate. This explains why so many people think that *boss* spelled backwards is double-S.O.B.

You can be the one to change this mind-set within your organization. All of it is worthless if you don't decide to lead. All of it goes to waste if your leadership is compromised, if you settle, if you don't commit. There is no reason why you should wait any longer. You can start right now.

....

"Great leaders don't focus on trying to get people to do something. They focus on trying to get people to be *something."*

....

Step Up

Most people are good followers, but many of them never learn to lead. They follow instructions, follow directions, and follow the pack. Although they may be consistently honing their skills, they're hiding. When people hide, it's because they are afraid. These people are every-where, in every profession—even in the fire service. Some people may ask the question, "What could a person who runs into burning buildings possibly be afraid of?" A firefighter will silently laugh at that question. Firefighters have fears, just like everyone else. Courage isn't the absence of fear. It's the management of fear.

Many people are afraid of failure. You may be one of them, but for most of us in the fire service, it's not failure that we fear, it's blame. No one likes to be criticized. I'll admit it. I don't like to be criticized. My first reaction is to defend myself. Most people are like me, but some allow their fear of criticism to prevent them from stepping up into a leadership role. They don't even like the thought that their actions may cause some form of criticism. So what do they do? Nothing (fig. 1–15)!

Fig. 1–15. Step up and take responsibility!

Becoming a leader requires going through some discomfort, which is exactly why we don't have more leaders than we do. If the pain of change is greater than the pain of staying the same, it's easy to fall back into a safe, obscure position. Leaders, on the other hand, are willing to get uncomfortable.

Leaders are willing to take a stand and challenge the status quo.

Leaders are willing to stand up in front of strangers.

Leaders are willing to give direction.

Leaders are willing to get uncomfortable.

Leaders are willing to be tough when they need to be.

Leaders are willing to tell someone when they're wrong.

Leaders are willing to praise someone when they do something right.

Leaders are willing to propose an idea that might fail.

Leaders are willing to take on the opposition when they know it's the right thing to do.

Leaders are willing to stop a destructive practice and start a new trend for the betterment of their organization.

In case you haven't figured it out, if you're not uncomfortable in your work as a leader, it's almost certain you're not reaching your potential as a leader. Too many people have been led to believe it's safe to do nothing—to get by. They think it is okay to just participate. While that may be the path that the masses choose, it's not the path for you. If it were, you wouldn't be reading this book.

On the pages that follow, I will introduce you to the core traits and skills that can be found among the top leaders within the fire service. Understanding these qualities helped me reach the top my profession (though I am still learning every day). I also used the skills I developed within the fire service to develop and lead a profitable sales team and launch a successful writing, consulting, and speaking career. My point is that it will benefit you to apply what you will learn in this book to any profession in which you are dealing with people on a daily basis, especially the fire service.

As you read the following chapters, you may find you are stronger in some areas than you are in others. This is expected. We all have strengths and weaknesses. What's important is that *you* are aware of what *your* strengths and weaknesses are. If you intend to lead others, you will need to know theirs as well. Becoming a leader is not as difficult as you may think. It's actually quite simple: Believe in something. Paint a clear picture of the future you want to create. Communicate your message to others. Utilize the talents and skills of those around you, and *step up and lead!*

2

LEADERSHIP TRAITS

Some people like to debate whether leaders are made or born. The most likely answer is that some true leaders are born, but most are made—self made. A smart firefighter will concentrate on developing the leadership qualities and traits that are necessary for success before becoming an officer. Receiving a promotion or bars on your collar doesn't automatically make you a leader. I have met knowledgeable officers (managers) who were ineffective leaders. This is common in all professions, including ours. As firefighters, we are constantly learning new skills in areas such as firefighting techniques, hazardous material response, technical rescue, and emergency medical treatment. Because the demand to perform is so high, fewer departments today are stressing the importance of personal growth. I believe this is a mistake.

I promise that you will never become a great leader if you don't take time to develop your people skills. So many of the problems we encounter in our professional lives are the result of an inability to deal with, motivate, and manage others (fig. 2–1). Trying to do so through fear and intimidation is weak. You may get people to work, but you will never get their best performance if you don't show them respect. You want to be respected, don't you? Well, so do the other people you work with. It would benefit you to try and imagine a sign around the neck of everyone you come in contact with that reads, "Make me feel important." A friend of mine is the CEO of a multi-million-dollar corporation. He lives by the words, "I see you, I hear you, what you say is important to me." Imagine treating people that way. Don't you think they would be more inclined to follow you?

Fig. 2–1. A leader's effectiveness will be largely determined by his ability to motivate others.

For the most part, leadership traits in all professions are universal. All great leaders should have vision, integrity, and the courage to communicate honestly. They need to be responsible and have the ability to empower others. Those traits are also important in the fire service. In our profession, however, there are specific qualities that an officer (or aspiring officer) absolutely must possess. In this chapter I introduce you to the most important leadership traits that firefighters—and the public—look for in a fire service leader. Firefighters who regularly demonstrate these leadership traits will earn the respect and confidence of their peers. By possessing these characteristics, you will make it easier for people to want to follow you. The less time you have to spend on getting others to follow you, the more time you get to spend refining exactly where you want to go and how to get there.

The acronym LEADERS TEACH was designed to help you remember these important traits (fig. 2–2).

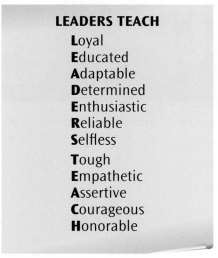

Fig. 2–2. Fire service leadership traits

On the following pages you will find definitions of each trait, followed by suggestions on how to develop the areas where you feel you are lacking (fig. 2–3). As you read each section, consistently ask yourself these three questions:

1. Which of the following traits do I possess?

2. Are others aware that I possess these traits?

3. Which ones do I need to work on?

Fig. 2–3. Leadership traits don't automatically come with a title and promotion.

Loyal

Have you ever met an elderly war veteran? Perhaps you were out having breakfast and he was sitting at the table next to you. A quick glance over and you immediately knew that person has served our country. How did you know? It's simple. He was wearing a shirt or hat, proudly displaying his association with one of our outstanding armed services.

I have often wondered how people who only spend a few precious years in the service proudly display loyalty to that organization for the rest of their lives. The reason is quite simple. Our armed services work hard to instill a set of core values. You have heard their mottos before, *"Once a Marine, always a Marine"* or *"There's strong, then there's . . ."* what? That's right *". . . Army strong."* That's pride, and with pride comes a certain degree of loyalty.

Firefighters are often the same way. They too are easy to spot on the street. A blue T-shirt with a Maltese cross is a firefighter's way of displaying loyalty—to a department, community, and the fire service as a whole. Some might say the fire service is the largest fraternity in the world. I happen to agree. And the Maltese cross is our crest.

If my car broke down and I saw a firehouse down the street, I'd knock on the door. You'd do the same thing. If you're out and you see someone wearing a fire department shirt, you immediately feel more comfortable around that person. The symbol is a sign of trust, respect, honor, and bravery. Loyalty, however, must go beyond simply wearing a T-shirt.

A firefighter has two families—the one at home, which ranks first, and the one at the firehouse. I find that those who have the strong family values and a solid foundation at home carry those values into their second family. The bottom line is that we need to take care of our families—plural. Firefighters who are leaders work hard to uphold the image of all firefighters.

Loyalty breeds pride in your job. Every morning, before the end of my shift, I would walk down the stairs to the apparatus floor and see the same thing: a firefighter from the incoming crew on top of the engine, checking the equipment and making sure all the tools were where they should be. His name is Kevin Becker. I have often told new firefighters on my shift to pay attention to what Kevin does when he walks into the firehouse. He immediately takes ownership of "his" engine. He talks to the driver of the previous shift and asks if anything was used or taken off the apparatus. Then he begins to get things ready for his watch. Kevin is loyal to the fire service. He is also very loyal to the other firefighters in his department. I have never heard him say one bad word about anyone. If he ever did have a problem with anyone, I never heard him say anything about it. I have a tremendous amount of respect for Kevin Becker and the loyalty he has displayed for the organization he works for (fig. 2–4).

Because the firehouse can sometimes feel like a fraternity, it's essential that you help create the right culture. Leaders don't disrespect coworkers when a person walks out of the room. Leaders know they are *not* better than anyone else. Leaders don't point fingers and blame. They are smart enough to know that when you point a finger at someone, there are three more on that same hand pointing back at you.

Fig. 2–4. Firefighter Kevin Becker is a loyal firefighter who treats the department's equipment as if it is his own.

As a leader in the fire service, I recognize how important it is that the public feels our loyalty toward them. If you are a firefighter, whether you realize it, you owe them. I know what you are thinking. I owe them? We are the ones who serve our community and run in when everyone else is running out. True, but firefighting is a privilege and customer service is an obligation. You have an obligation to provide the *best* service possible. Doing so means you are loyal to your customers. This can be the simple act of shaking hands with someone before you leave the scene of a minor incident, such as a malfunctioning smoke alarm. The key to customer service is connecting with people. We discuss this more thoroughly in chapter 4.

With loyalty comes commitment. A committed firefighter is accountable to other firefighters, other officers, and mentors. You don't have to be the highest-ranking officer or the most powerful person in the room to be a leader. However, you *do* have to be committed. You *do* have to be loyal.

....

"The strength of a family, like the strength
of an army, is in its loyalty to each other."

....

Summary

Being loyal means you are devoted to your organization, your community, and your team. Loyalty should flow evenly, up and down the chain of command, to seniors, subordinates, and peers. To be loyal is to be dependable and trustworthy, which means that you can be relied on to perform your duties properly and trusted to complete your assignment every time.

Suggestions for improvement

Refrain from discussing the problems of the organization with outsiders. Never talk about superior officers or those in managerial positions unfavorably in front of your subordinates. Also, carry out every task to the best of your ability regardless of whether you like or agree with it. Once a decision is made, and you are given an order to execute it, carry out that order willingly as if it were your own decision.

Educated

When I was in the fire academy, I had an instructor named Mike Terpak. He was a firefighter from Jersey City, one of the busiest departments in New Jersey, and he clearly had an extreme amount of passion for the job. Mike taught me how to do things like connect to a hydrant, tie knots, advance a hose line, and raise a ladder. He was the first person I heard say the words, "The day you stop learning is the day you need to retire." Throughout the years I stayed in touch with Mike and watched him advance his career to the rank of deputy chief. One day, about fifteen years into my career, I called him, and guess what he was doing . . . reading a fire service book.

I began to take classes with him, and although I didn't tell him, I began to try to emulate his habits. Mike Terpak became my mentor in the fire service. One of my proudest professional accomplishments has been to coauthor a bestselling fire service textbook with him, titled *Fireground Operational Guides*.

Those who have ever attended one of Chief Terpak's classes will be familiar with the saying, "You have to know your enemy." He would say that, referring to the importance of learning about building construction (fig. 2–5).

Fig. 2–5. Deputy Chief Mike Terpak teaching a class on building construction at a FireOpsOnline Seminar in New Jersey

Building construction is just one of *many* areas a firefighter must learn about. A fire service leader's job is to make good decisions. You cannot do that without an education. Unfortunately, there are not many tests a firefighter will have to take after the academy. This can cause some people to become complacent, which is extremely dangerous in our profession. The fact that you are reading this book shows that you do not fall into that category. I commend you for that. A true leader understands that self-education is essential regardless of a person's chosen profession.

The three best ways to learn in any profession are through reading books, attending seminars, and on-the-job training. In the fire service's case, the fourth best way of learning is by conducting a post-incident analysis (PIA) after real-world incidents. We obviously can't schedule fires, so we have no control over how many fires or incidents we will respond to; however, we do have a responsibility to conduct PIAs after any large-scale or unusual incident. We do have total control over the other three ways we learn. Let's break them down one by one.

Books

Why do so many wait for a promotional cycle before they open a book? Leaders know better. They stay on top of their game. They are constantly looking for ways to better themselves. They understand that complacency kills. Complacency may not be life threatening in other professions, but it is in ours. There is an easy, 15-minute-per-day solution. If you spend 15 minutes every day in an educational book, that compounds to 5,475 minutes a year. That's more than 90 hours a year you have spent improving and educating yourself. Now compound that over the next ten years. You can see how the correct, small, daily actions can produce incredible results. This is called the compound effect, and it applies to leadership in all professions, not just ours. There is no shortage of books for you to pick up and take advantage of. There is, however, a shortage of dedicated leaders who take advantage of every resource they can get their hands on. Mark Twain once said, "The person who *does not* read good books has no advantage over the person who *cannot*." Those are strong words, and accurate ones.

Seminars

Associating with other dedicated and accomplished people in your field is another great way to advance your skills. I encourage all young firefighters to be smart enough to surround themselves with educated firefighters. They are easy to find. They are usually the ones spending an occasional Saturday at a local fire academy or seminar learning from specialists in their field (figs. 2–6 and 2–7). I have always found that attending seminars provided me with two great opportunities: (1) to expand my knowledge base and (2) to network with like-minded people. I always enjoy pressing palms with my brothers and sisters and exchanging information. This has led to some of my most treasured relationships in the industry. When I was the training officer for my department, I would constantly call up other training officers I met in seminars and share information about grants, SOPs, training tips, and anything else I (or they) had questions about. We would bounce ideas off each other and learn from each of our experiences. It all came from attending events.

On-the-job training

This is clearly one of the most important ways to learn. Firefighting is arguably the most dangerous job on earth. I'm sure there are many other dangerous professions, and I am certainly not minimizing any of them. For example, you'll never see me moonlighting as a lion tamer in a traveling circus. I am only speaking about what I know. Firefighters may be placed in a life-threatening situation at any given moment, without warning. Because of this, we must do everything in our power to make sure we protect ourselves and the men and women around us. A firefighter should never become complacent with essential equipment like personal protective equipment and self-contained breathing apparatus. Firefighters are expected to train regularly on things they think they know as well as areas where they know they are lacking. Be willing to learn. Don't hesitate to ask questions. If you haven't been assigned a mentor, ask someone you respect to mentor you. Then, when the time is right, step up and mentor others. I will discuss mentoring programs in the next chapter. For now, I'd like to sum it up with the words of my mentor, Chief Terpak, "The day you stop learning is the day you need to retire."

Figs. 2–6 and 2–7. Educated firefighters are easy to find. They are usually the ones spending an occasional Saturday at a fire seminar, listening to experts, and associating with like-minded people.

The public expects firefighters to be jacks of all trades and masters of them all. We have the obligation to do everything in our power not to let the public down. We are still killing more than 100 firefighters a year and injuring tens of thousands in spite of having better apparatus, equipment, and turnout gear than we had in the past. Yes, construction and contents are different, but fire doesn't burn any hotter today than it did 20 years ago. It is what it has always been. We cannot become complacent. A leader will take the initiative to train on safety and survival skills such as Mayday, ladder carries, and emergency bailout. A leader will practice SCBA maneuvers and rapid intervention techniques.

We need to learn from the past, but we can't afford to live in it. If you want to be a leader, make the decision that you are going to learn something new *every day*!

....

"It's better to be lucky rather than smart,

but if you're smart, you have a better

chance of being lucky"

—*Vincent Dunn, FDNY*

....

Summary

Being educated means that you continue to acquire appropriate information from reliable sources and that you understand your duties, the policies and procedures of your organization, and the science of firefighting. Your education should be broad, and you should *never* stop trying to improve your knowledge base. The day you think you know too much is the day you should consider retiring. In the fire service, we have a saying: "The biggest room in the fire station is the room for improvement."

Suggestions for improvement

Increase your knowledge by committing to continual learning and remaining alert. Constantly listen, observe, and learn about things you don't understand. Read textbooks, attend educational seminars, talk to people who are great at your profession, and ask questions. There is an endless supply of knowledge available. You just have to seek it.

Adaptable

Years ago, a person became a firefighter and did just that: fought fires. Today, firefighters understand that they do much more than put the wet stuff on the hot stuff. It doesn't take long for the modern-day firefighter to recognize that the job description has expanded to hazardous material first responder, emergency medical technician, extrication specialist, technical rescue expert (fig. 2–8), and a weapons-of-mass-destruction first responder who is positioned on the forefront of America's fight against terrorism. This is all in addition to the plumbing, electrical, and building construction knowledge we must have. Not to mention carbon monoxide and fire investigation knowledge.

After seven years on the job, I reached the rank of captain and was chosen to be the head of our training division. This was the result of a very careful and thorough selection process on behalf of my department. That process went something like this—no one else wanted to do it! I received the job by default. I was the junior guy. I remember our administrative deputy chief walking up to me and asking if I would be interested in the job. My exact reply was, "What does it entail?" Apparently, that one innocent question was all it took. He later told me that I was the one who showed the most interest. Needless to say, I was not happy, but I embraced the challenge and looked at it as a way to grow and improve myself. Within a few years, I had developed 50 general operating guidelines (our version of standard operating procedures) and hundreds of training-related documents, some of which my department still uses today.

Fig. 2–8. Most fire departments doing technical rescue today were not equipped or trained to do so 10 or 20 years ago.

Maybe you are currently working as your organization's training officer. You might even be called upon to become a grant writer, like I was. Heck, I didn't even know if I had the ability to write the way a grant writer does. It was yet another challenge, but I accepted. Five years later, I had secured close to $3 million in grant money . . . and I still didn't consider myself a very talented grant writer. How is it that a person who takes a job as a firefighter ends up adding grant writer to his job description? The answer is simple: as firefighters, we adapt.

When I became the training officer on my department—even though I didn't have a choice—everyone said I was crazy. They complained that the workload was unappealing. I couldn't disagree at first. They even said I wouldn't be able to study for promotional exams in that position because of the work schedule. Again, I couldn't disagree, but in spite of the unappealing workload and inability to study, I managed to reach the rank of deputy chief and write four books (to date). Why? Because I adapted. *You* can adapt too. To be a leader you must.

You already adapt, but is it by choice? In other words, do you adapt because you have to, or because you are a leader who is looking for the *one best way* to accomplish a specific task? That's the objective behind standard operating procedures (SOPs). An SOP is developed to inform others what is the one best way to operate. Your organization may have a book of SOPs (hopefully you do), and those SOPs should be followed. However, the fireground is complex and unpredictable. It's ever changing. Because of that, a leader in the fire service must be able to adapt and make tough decisions without hesitation.

Being adaptable means you are able to adjust quickly to rapidly changing conditions. This trait is paramount for all firefighters because situations escalate quickly on the fireground (fig. 2–9). I have said it a thousand times, but the fact is there are only two ways to put out a fire—out-resource it or out-think it. In today's fire service, it's becoming more and more difficult to out-resource a fire. You have to be able to out-think it and then adapt. Your ability to evaluate and revise your strategies on the fly is imperative to your overall success.

Fig. 2–9. Being adaptable and able to adjust your strategy quickly is a paramount trait for firefighters because situations escalate quickly on the fireground.

To be adaptable, you must also be resourceful. Being resourceful means you are capable of skillfully, safely, and promptly navigating your way through a variety of situations, regardless of the tools, staffing, and resources that are—or aren't—available at any given moment. If you are resourceful, you are creative, and you will always be looked at as a person with ingenuity who shows initiative and can get the job done, no matter what. Sure, you and I may never be able to stop an acid leak with a chocolate bar like MacGyver did in the 1980s, but we can prepare ourselves to tackle the challenges that are thrown at us. Look at it this way: if your supervisor continues to throw stuff on your lap, you must be talented, determined, or both.

Don't ever lose sight of the fact that the only time you grow is when you step outside of your comfort zone. You may be confident in your abilities on the fireground. You may have no problem running into the type of structure that even other firefighters may think twice about entering, but you suddenly find yourself having to take on an administrative task that scares the heck out of you. My advice is to tackle that task with vigor. That's what a leader would do. The truth is that we should never feel too comfortable in our job. A firefighter who feels comfortable enough in his or her career to sit back and relax is a danger to everyone.

....

"Today's leaders are expected to both anticipate problems and meet them as they come."

....

Summary

Being adaptable means you are able to adjust quickly to rapidly changing conditions. This trait is paramount for all firefighters because situations escalate quickly on the fireground. A "routine" fire can turn into a life-threatening situation in seconds, which is why there is no such thing as a routine fire. Your ability to evaluate and revise your strategies on the fly is imperative. An adaptable firefighter is resourceful and can skillfully, safely, and promptly navigate his or her way through a variety of situations, regardless of the tools, staffing, and resources that are—or aren't—available at any given moment.

Suggestions for improvement

Again, never stop educating yourself. The more you know, the better equipped you will be to react and adjust, practice being proactive, not reactive. The more capable you are at seeing problems before they happen, the more effective you will be in your chosen field. To adapt, you must learn to think outside of the box. Don't get tunnel vision. There are always alternative ways to accomplish a task. To be able to make tough decisions quickly, you must also work on staying mentally and physically alert.

Determined

The word *determined*, in the context of firefighting, is synonymous with *heroic*. To be determined means you have the end goal in mind and you will not stop, quit, or slow down until you have achieved that goal. Our profession involves risk, so it needs to be stressed that a proper risk assessment must take place. Every firefighter in the country should have the following saying (or a variation of it) posted on the wall:

We risk a lot to save savable lives.

We risk little to save savable property.

We risk nothing to save lives and property already lost.

Once that risk assessment is understood, we can talk more about determination. A true leader has vision. Leaders clearly see the end result, and they are able to communicate that goal to others. Setting a goal is essential, but that's the easy part. Following through is the hard part.

When things become difficult, if a person does not have determination, the obstacles will become greater than the desire to succeed. This can be dangerous on the fireground. A leader will instill the proper mind set into his team: "Give us a challenge. We *will* face it and we *will* overcome!"

Look around. Everywhere you look you will see problem finders. They are on the news, in your neighborhood, and maybe even sitting in managerial positions within your organization. There is no room in the fire service for problem finders. We need problem *solvers*. I have often told my group, "I don't mind if you bring a problem into my office, but you better bring a solution along with it." Why? Because that's what we do. When someone is trapped inside a burning building, we are there to solve the problem. When a man needs to be extricated from a vehicle, we are there to solve the problem (fig. 2–10). When a woman calls because she smells an odor of gas in her house, we are there to solve the problem. It's not enough to just show up, we must show up, determined!

Fig. 2–10. Determined firefighters work to extricate a driver from his vehicle.

In 2003, I wrote the book *Common Valor: True Stories from New Jersey's Bravest*. My original thought was to write about heroic stories that had never been documented. I decided to do this by interviewing the firefighters to hear what happened in their own words. It didn't take long for me to realize that the book was about more than bravery; it was about determination. I remember sitting down with an officer named Chris Weiss from the East Orange Fire Department as he said the following words to me, "The victim and I were lying face to face with each other in the hallway. They were smothering the fire on his leg, but we made it out and he was alive. I was exhausted. I wanted to be done. Then he looked at me and he said, "But the baby, what about the baby?"

Chris was mentally and physically exhausted, but he picked himself up and forced his way through the flames to find the baby inside the apartment. There is only one word to describe this—*determination*.

Is it possible to be too determined? Yes, especially in our profession. Sometimes, we are determined to a fault. More than once it was a brother's determination that led to his paying the ultimate price, which is why I started this section with risk assessment, and I am repeating that message again. A leader is determined, but also safe, smart, and calculated in his or her actions.

Determination enables you to create good habits. When wanting to accomplish a certain goal—such as improving the time it takes to set up a relay pump operation—a firefighter will discuss that goal with the crew, work out a game plan, then train consistently until that goal is reached. You will do this by developing a mechanism for evaluating your progress. Once the proper habits are developed, any realistic goal can be achieved by following that same format. The same can be said about work around the firehouse and administrative tasks. Nothing great will ever be accomplished without a determination to succeed. The way a fire service leader sets and tackles goals around the fire station and on the training ground will be similar to the way he or she (and the crew) will operate when the call comes in.

....

"We will either find a way, or make one!"

—*Hannibal*

....

Summary

Being determined means you have laser-sharp focus on the goal you are trying to achieve. There's a saying: "Brick walls aren't there to keep you out, they're there to see how badly you want to get in." That's the way an aggressive, strong-minded firefighter will think when performing a duty on the fireground. The word *determined*, in the context of firefighting, is synonymous with *heroic*.

Suggestions for improvement

Never, ever, give up. Don't just say you want to do something. Set goals, develop a strong work ethic, create the proper habits, and don't quit until the goal has been achieved. This does not mean you should ever defy your supervisor (or the incident commander's orders on the fireground) if there is a need to change tactics. Proper risk assessment must trump your determination level. It simply means that when firefighters say they risk a lot to save lives, they don't just say it . . . they live it.

Enthusiastic

All firefighters remember their first week on the job. Sure they were nervous, but they were also full of zeal and excitement, eager to learn and ready to take on the world. I'm sure you were also passionate about your new job title and full of pride. In short, you were enthusiastic.

Are you still enthusiastic about what you do?

One evening, I was sitting at the kitchen table talking with the newest probie on my shift. He was asking questions about how things *used to be*. I talked about our pull-up boots and open cab engines. I spoke about job security then compared to now; although he was only on the job a year, there was already talk in town about possible layoffs and demotions. After talking about the good, the bad, and the uncertain future of the fire service, I ended with, "After 21 years in the fire service, I can tell you with 100% certainty that this is absolutely the best job on earth" (fig. 2–11).

Fig. 2–11. It's common for firefighters to agree that we have the best job on earth.

Enthusiasm comes from having a passion for what you do. An enthusiastic leader with passion and few skills will always outperform a leader with great skills and no passion. I once read that 3% of what you say to someone is in the form of your words. Ninety-seven percent of what you say comes from how you say those words. If I walk past a group of firefighters with my shoulders slumped and mumble the words, "Let's go out and train," without making eye contact, how do you think they are going to feel? Unenthusiastic, I'm sure. Now, imagine I walk up to those same firefighters, eagerly smack my hands together, and excitedly say those same five words. Although the words are the same, the message is completely different.

A good leader will inspire people to have confidence in his or her leadership. A great leader will inspire people to have confidence in themselves. One way to do this is to make noise. What do I mean? There are more positive people on the job than negative; the negative ones just seem to make more noise. That's one of the reasons why morale will begin to drop. If you are enthusiastic, you must *make noise*. Enthusiasm is one of the best tools you can use to help motivate others.

Be enthusiastic about the job and your vision. When dealing with problems, if you need to talk with someone about the right way to handle a situation, talk to an equal or higher-ranking individual. There will be times you encounter challenges, concerns, anger, and frustration. Remember this simple phrase: negative up, positive down. Don't spread negative down to the members you are leading. They don't have to think you have *all* the answers—you don't—but they do have to have confidence in you. If you panic or lose control, there is a good chance they will do the same.

Firefighters must also always remember to respect the chain of command. When you need to approach a superior with a problem, only go as high as the next level of command. If you bring a problem, show that you are a leader by also bringing a possible solution. That's what leaders do. They solve problems.

Don't ever criticize, condemn, or complain just for the sake of it. When you do that, you are showing signs of weakness as a leader. Your job is always to be looking to make things better. If you feel like you are coasting or maintaining the status quo, you are really just losing momentum. The next phase is rolling downhill. You can prevent this from occurring by taking control. And the only thing you have complete control over is your attitude. Attitudes are contagious. Ask yourself the question, *Is mine worth catching?*

If you are a fire service officer, don't forget where you came from. Keep the enthusiasm that drove you to the rank you have attained. That same passion can help you become an effective leader. Enthusiasm keeps people engaged. Remember the speech that Mel Gibson's character William Wallace gave in the movie *Braveheart*? How about the one Kurt Russell's character Herb Brooks gave in the movie *Miracle*? Both are examples of passion, drive, and enthusiasm. No one is saying you have to prepare a pre-game speech every time an alarm comes in. You would be wise, however, to approach every task (around the firehouse and in the field) with the right attitude.

Use your enthusiasm as a springboard. Do more than is required of you. Aim higher than the others around you are. Try harder than you did yesterday. Be grateful for things you have overlooked for too long. Don't manage, *lead*. Managers are cynical. Managers are pessimists because they've seen it before and believe they've already done it as well as it can be done. Leaders, on the other hand, are enthusiastic about positive change. Without that, there is no future to work toward.

....

"Enthusiasm will take you further

than talent, title, or skill."

—*Robin Crow*

....

Summary

Enthusiasm is defined as a sincere interest and exuberance in the performance of your duties. If you are enthusiastic, you are optimistic, cheerful, and willing to accept challenges. You are the type of person who is eager to take on more responsibility. Every organization and team needs more leaders with this trait, because enthusiasm is contagious.

Suggestions for improvement

Understanding and believing in the mission of your organization will add to your enthusiasm for the job. In the fire service, our mission is to reduce the loss of life and property and protect the weak. To do this, everyone will have to fulfill a role on the fireground. Because of this, it's important to understand why even the uninteresting jobs must be done with the proper attitude.

Reliable

When I was growing up, my father was at every soccer game, football game, wrestling match, and crew meet I ever competed in. When I needed advice, my father was always there for me. When people ask me to describe my father, I use the words honest, trustworthy, and reliable.

At age 29 my father joined the Kearny Fire Department (NJ). He spent 30 years in the profession. He had a passion for the job and a desire to help others. Anyone who worked with my father would describe him as . . . you guessed it: honest, trustworthy, and reliable (fig. 2–12).

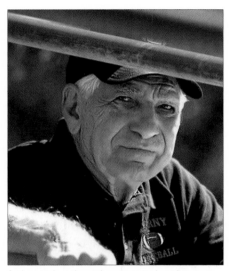

Fig. 2–12. This is my father Sebastian Viscuso. My brother Joe and I never had to look hard to find a perfect example of reliability.

Reliability cannot be faked. If you are a reliable parent, you will be a reliable employee. If you are unorganized and fail to meet important deadlines in your personal life, you are likely to be the same way in your professional life. Like all the other traits, this takes work, but anyone can become reliable.

To further expand on this thought, reliability in the firehouse is just as important as reliability on the fireground. If a firefighter cuts corners or can't be counted on to take out the garbage, wash the apparatus, or complete reports in time, how would that firefighter expect to be considered reliable at a structure fire? Reliability is the ability of a person to perform and maintain his or her functions in routine circumstances as well as hostile or unexpected circumstances. The way others judge you (and yes, others are always judging you) is by how you respond and function on a daily basis. If I ask you to do something, even as simple as mopping the floor, and a hour goes by without this task being started, my immediate thought would be that you are not reliable. If you can't do a simple task, why would I think you are my go-to person on the fireground? I also expect the group of firefighters I lead to hold me equally as accountable in that respect.

As a fire service leader, being reliable means people—your community, customers, and coworkers—can count on you to get the job done, every time. If you are assigned to the truck and the incident commander says, "I need ventilation, now!" He needs to know you are on it (fig. 2–13). If you are the first-arriving engine company officer and you upgrade the assignment to a second alarm before a chief officer arrives on scene, everyone responding to that incident should know you made that call for a reason. Your actions and judgment are reliable. Maybe you have only been on the job for two months and you haven't been able to prove that you are reliable. Now is the time to start. When given a task, no matter how small, do it, and do it well. By the way, if you have in fact been on the job for only two months, congratulations for reading this book. That's a great sign that your head is in the right place.

Fig. 2–13. Reliable firefighters don't wait for conditions to be perfect. They can be counted on to get the job done regardless of what is happening around them.

Another trait that falls in line with reliability is integrity. Integrity is all-encompassing. A leader may be weak in other traits, but without rock-solid integrity, his or her leadership is a house of cards. Let's not beat around the bush. Ask 10 different people to define integrity, and you may get 10 variations. Here is mine: "Integrity is what you do when no one is watching."

When we talk about being reliable under normal and/or hostile circumstances, we should also mention the importance of initiative. It's great to be the person who can be counted on when assigned a task, but it's better to be the person who doesn't need to be told what to do. You already know what needs to be done, and you already know how to do it, so you take the initiative and get the job done. Kevin Donnelly is this type of officer. When I was assigned my shift, I was told that a few firefighters on that shift had a difficult time working with Kevin. He was an officer with as much time on the job as I had, and I knew he was knowledgeable. I was curious why these men, good firefighters within their own right, had issues with him. It didn't take long for me to find out. Kevin didn't need to be told what to do. He just did it. What firefighters may have seen as a challenge, I saw as a tremendous asset. Anytime I needed something done, I called on Kevin. I can remember conversations that went something like this. I would say, "Cap, It's been a long time since we had an extrications drill. Later today I am going to call around and see if I can get us a car we can drill with on our next day in." Kevin would respond with, "I'll take a drive down to the towing yard now and see if they have one for us. If they do, would you like us to do the drill today instead of next tour?" One hour later, Kevin would have his crew tearing up a car. One month later, Kevin would come up to me and say, "Chief, if it's okay with you, I'm going to try and secure another vehicle so we can do another extrication drill."

How could I possibly have a problem with that type of initiative? I found out that the main reason the individuals had issues with him was because they felt he would often schedule last-minute drills. Once I explained to them that he did that because he wanted to get things done immediately so there was no procrastination, they agreed it was a good quality. I have no problem going on record saying that Captain Donnelly is exactly what I like to see in a company officer. He makes great decisions and is reliable in the firehouse and on the fireground. He is a talented firefighter who knows how to get the job done.

....

*"If you can't be counted on to take out the garbage,
wash the apparatus, or complete your reports
on time, how do you expect to be considered
reliable at a structure fire?"*

....

Summary

In general, reliability is the ability of a person to perform and maintain his or her functions in routine circumstances as well as hostile or unexpected circumstances. As firefighters we routinely work in hostile circumstances, so this trait is especially essential. As a fire service leader, being reliable means people—your community, customers, and coworkers—can count on you to get the job done, every time.

Suggestions for improvement

Learn how to do your job the best you possibly can and train daily. Become proficient in your skills, and take initiative to tackle and complete projects and assignments. Determine in your mind that you are going to become one of your organization's go-to guys or gals. Then verbalize that commitment to the management and superiors within your organization. If they are quality leaders, they will appreciate your desire to do and be more.

Selfless

Why do people become firefighters? They certainly aren't doing it for the money. If you are a career firefighter, you already know you won't become rich in this profession, which is why most firefighters have side jobs. Yes, we make a comfortable living, and don't get me wrong, the pay isn't terrible. I'm only stating the fact that there is a much more meaningful reason why the majority of firefighters take the job than a paycheck.

Firefighting is a selfless job. You have taken an oath to risk your life for complete strangers. When the call comes in and you jump on the apparatus, you have no idea what you are responding to or what you may be called upon to do. Lenny Calvo of North Hudson Regional Fire and Rescue understands this completely. If there was any doubt in his mind, that doubt disappeared the day he responded to a major fire in a 20-story apartment complex and climbed up to a fourth-floor balcony just to put himself between a raging fire and a woman who was unable to escape. Using his body as a human shield was a selfless act. The same can be said about my friend and coworker Robert Osborn. When "Ozzie" was driving around town, off duty, and he came across a house fire, he didn't think twice. Without the protection of personal protective gear, an SCBA, or a hose line, he valiantly ran deep into the smoke-charged structure to rescue an unconscious man and woman. Again, a selfless act. These stories happen regularly in the fire service.

To be a leader, you have to take it one step further than what happens on the fireground. Leaders are selfless in all areas. Real leaders don't care about getting the credit. *Anyone* can find the negatives. When dealing with others, especially those you work with, look for the positives. It's okay to catch someone doing something right. And when you do, it's okay to offer praise for it. And when you do praise someone for a job well done, be sure to do it in front of others. When you look for the positives, the negatives tend to fade away.

As a leader, your job is to help others develop confidence, especially during tough times. As Napoleon Bonaparte said, "Leaders are dealers in hope." That confidence comes in part from believing in your team. But believing in people alone is not enough. You have to help them succeed. If your team succeeds, you succeed. That last sentence is one that I wish every person in a leadership position understood. Since you are the one reading this book, you are now aware of one of the top reasons why teams fail: so-called "leaders" who want to take all the credit.

Too many people in leadership positions are too in love with their own ideas and don't know how to distribute credit. A strong leader in any profession thinks differently. Once a week, New Orleans Saints quarterback Drew Brees took his Super Bowl champion offensive line out to dinner to thank them for keeping the opposing team from making roadkill out of him. Sports commentators would praise the quarterback for the big numbers he was throwing up. In the 2011 season, he broke Dan Marino's single-season passing record. Brees responded by praising his teammates. "I only throw the ball," he said, "I wouldn't have accomplished much if there wasn't someone on the other end catching it." That same year, New York Jets head coach Rex Ryan told his players that any time they are giving an interview, they have to mention at least two other players and one coach. That's great advice. Get so good at distributing recognition to others that you don't have time to seek it for yourself.

There's no record of Martin Luther King Jr. or Ronald Regan whining about not getting enough credit. That's because there is paradox to leadership. To be an important leader, you have to be the least important person on the team. Remember, if you want to take credit for when things go right, you'd also have to be willing to take blame for when things go wrong. Ah, suddenly taking all the credit doesn't seem like a great idea after all. What if you shared the credit? How would that change the dynamics of your department or team? True leaders are selfless and recognize others for their achievements. They understand that recognition is the fuel that drives the engine.

The key to success is to work less as an individual and more as a team (fig. 2–14). This brings me to a leadership technique called the Lane Theory. The concept is simple. Everyone has a specialty—a strength. Your job is to identify a person's strength and make use of it. There is so much talent in the fire service. So many members are carpenters, plumbers, electricians, and even successful business owners with managerial and organization skills. Some are great researchers, some have tremendous communications skills, and others want the toughest job on the fireground and will not be happy with anything less. A fire service leader's job is to identify a person's strength and utilize that strength often. Don't expect everyone to be great at everything. Albert Einstein once said, "Everyone is a genius. But if you judge a fish on its ability to climb a tree, it will live its whole life believing that it is stupid." Again, your job is to identify and utilize.

Fig. 2–14. The key to success is to work less as an individual and more as a team.

If you are surrounded by talented people, they should know you feel that way about them. Let them know when they do a good job. A great fire service leader will be more interested in putting a letter of commendation in a firefighter's personnel file than a letter of reprimand. A great leader says "Great job!" and "Thank you!" as often as possible. A great leader doesn't brag about personal accomplishments. A great leader brags about the team.

There is one caveat to the Lane Theory. Although you should recognize the talents of others, don't fall in love with their "potential." More time is wasted trying to motivate people with "potential" than just about anything else in most industries. Instead, spend most of your energy with people who are passionate, hungry, and motivated. Doing so will help keep you energized as well.

Firefighting is a very serious job, but as firefighters we don't have to take ourselves so seriously that we make a difficult working environment for those around us. Don't forget that the firefighters you respond with are the ones who will risk their lives to save you. They deserve your respect, and you deserve theirs.

Think about this, why does society mainly honor people after they're gone? The fire service has great traditions. Among them are promotional ceremonies, award ceremonies, and retirement parties. These traditions need to be preserved. Honoring people who are still with us is better than paying tribute to them when they're gone.

We are talking about the right way to manage people, but how do you manage leaders? The answer is quite simple. Find them and support them. And don't ever forget, it's amazing how much you can accomplish when you let others get the credit they deserve.

....

"A great leader never sets himself above his followers except in carrying responsibilities."

—*Jules Ormont*

....

Summary

The true definition of the word *selfless* is having little or no concern for oneself. Firefighting is arguably the most selfless job on the planet. It's our job to put the safety and well-being of others ahead of our own. Although selflessness has a lot to do with *self-sacrifice*, this doesn't mean a firefighter should disregard safe practices. To be selfless also means you are considerate of others and openly give credit to those who deserve it.

Suggestions for improvement

Think more about others and less about yourself. Avoid using your position or rank for personal gain, safety, or pleasure at the expense of others. Be considerate of those you work with and give credit where credit is due. It's amazing how much your team can accomplish when you praise often and in public and give other people the credit they deserve.

Tough

I first met Bryan Emenecker in 2011. He was speaking at a fire service seminar about search techniques (fig. 2–15). He immediately impressed me, not just with his knowledge about the job, but also with his compelling stories about his time on the front line with his brothers. Bryan was a captain on the Camden Fire Department, one of the busiest departments in the state. Camden held the distinction of being named one the most dangerous cities in the United States. That title was bestowed upon it before the city cut its police force in half due in part to a recession and in part to political posturing. After the class, I spent time talking with Bryan, and he told me that his department, which was also being affected by cuts and restructuring, was battling vacant and abandoned warehouse fires on a weekly (and sometimes daily) basis.

Fig. 2–15. Camden Fire Captain Bryan Emenecker

Although he was a Philadelphia Flyers fan and I liked the New Jersey Devils (and anyone who was playing the Flyers), we still had a lot in common, and we became friends. (Again, I can't stress enough how important it is to network and associate with like-minded people.) The more I learned about Bryan, the more impressed I was. Here was a guy who liked to work out . . . with Navy Seals. The way he was built, I'm sure a lot of those Seals had to work as hard to keep up with him as he did to stay on pace with them.

What I liked the most about Bryan is his *all chips in* attitude: "We want the hardest job on the fireground and we want it every time." When I describe him to other firefighters, I often say, "He's the real deal." They immediately know what I mean. He's a tough guy who is ready to take on anything. Bryan is the type of guy who has the tenacity of a pit bull on the fireground. Let's just say he has earned more than a few trips to the local burn center.

Although Bryan is about 225 pounds of muscle, he is not the toughest guy I have ever met. I'm pretty sure the toughest guy I have ever met is one of my neighbors. He only weighs 150 pounds and doesn't look very tough at all. However, from April 2010 to February 2012, he was the Ultimate Fighting Championships lightweight title holder. His name is Frankie Edgar. Just watch one of the fights between Frankie and Gray Maynard in 2011 and you will see why I give him props. Frankie is a real-life *Rocky* movie. I encourage my boys to watch his fights every time they are televised. All of us can find inspiration by the person who keeps getting knocked down but refuses to stay down. For me, that inspiration came in the form of a 150-pound fighter from Toms River, New Jersey.

Toughness comes in all shapes and sizes. It doesn't matter what race or religion you are. It doesn't matter what gender or age you are. It doesn't matter how big or small you are . . . what matters is the size of your heart. Tough leaders love the fight itself. To them, it's not about winning or losing (although we all want to win). The real reward comes from the ability to endure great strain without breaking. Although I am talking about physical and mental toughness, it isn't just about your ability to take a punch, or your willingness to take on the hardest job on the fireground. It's also about being willing to make tough decisions.

You can be a buddy, but make the conscious choice to be a leader first and a buddy second. There will be times when you have to address difficult situations, such as insubordination. There may also be times when the individual in question is a friend of yours. This can be one of the most difficult situations a leader in the fire service will encounter, but you have to be able to put personal feeling aside and do what needs to be done. This means making tough decisions.

In the next chapter, I offer some suggestions on how to manage people following the 3U method. That may help you determine how to handle a situation, but it still doesn't make it easy. I have told my crew that I am Frank around the firehouse (although they all address me as Chief), but on the fireground, and any time a situation happens where I have to take action, I am no longer Frank. I'm Deputy Chief Viscuso. They completely understand that. As a result, we have had a great working environment without any major problems.

The one thing you should always keep in mind is that people *want* someone to lead them. When I took command of my shift, I told the officers that I wanted to train for no fewer than three hours a day. This is in addition to all the housework, incidents, and other daily duties. At first I thought they were going to be resistant. However, I was happy to see they were not only willing to train often, they were happy that I gave them a definitive guide to follow. Three hours, minimum, no matter what.

....

"You never will be the person you can be, if pressure, tension, and discipline are taken out of your life."

—*Herbert Bayard Swope*

....

My brother Joe is also a deputy chief, and he set a similar standard. One time he told his members to do a specific drill. After the sun went down, he was aggravated when he found out the drill had not been completed. Instead of yelling, he made a tough decision. At 10:00 in the evening, he told the officers to assemble the men and head down to the drill site. He then said, "If you don't do it on your time, you will have to do it on my time." He never had a problem after that. It was a tough decision, but it paid off in the end.

Summary

To be tough is to be strong and resilient, able to withstand adverse conditions. With toughness comes the ability to endure great strain without breaking. This means both physically and mentally, and it's a necessity for firefighters of all ranks. There is nothing easy about fighting fires. If you aren't tough, this simply isn't the right profession for you.

Suggestions for improvement

You have to learn to love the fight itself. Champions in every arena love to compete. However, it is vitally important to cultivate your love of the fight more than your love of winning. This way of thinking will help improve your mental toughness. Improving your physical toughness will come from a consistent workout program.

Empathetic

This book was written during a time when most Americans would agree that one of our country's top moral problems is our mutual lack of respect, compassion, and consideration for others. Many politicians and people in leadership positions fail in these basic areas of human need. The members of the fire service are famous for providing great service and for promoting family values. We love our family, and we love our brothers and sisters. But a *true* leader will also love the public. Not just because they pay for our apparatus and salary and benefits, but because a true leader understands that we are servants (fig. 2–16).

Fig. 2–16. Firefighters are the epitome of public servants.

Strategically, the first five minutes of an incident are the most important. That is when we determine our initial strategy and place our hose lines. Fortunately, if a mistake is made, there is a trump card— the last five minutes. How you treat the public can decide the fate of your organization.

I respectfully ask you to read that last paragraph again. It's vitally important. If your desire is to be a leader in your profession, you must understand how essential it is to show empathy for others. I remember back in 1996, the members of our department had just become EMTs, and we had taken on the added duties of first responders. I had only been on several EMS calls when we received one for an attempted suicide. I didn't know what to expect, which made me a bit nervous. When I got off the engine, a cop met us at the front door and said, "Be careful, she's carrying." I didn't know what he meant by that so I looked at Henry Magee. He was the veteran firefighter on duty that day. Henry looked at me and said one word, "AIDS."

I was a new EMT and didn't know much about HIV or AIDS. Of course I knew about universal precautions, but there was still a great fear about this relatively new virus at that time. As we entered the house, my anxiety turned into a silent panic when we found a razor blade in the bathroom. The walls were stained with blood. The floor was completely covered. Footprints went from the bathroom to the bedroom. Henry followed the trail and found a woman in her early thirties sitting on the edge of her bed. Her forearms were sliced multiple times. My heart started pounding. I was wondering if we should wait for the paramedics and let them handle it. Henry had completely different response than I did. He walked over to the bed, and sat down on the end. Facing the woman, he grabbed her hands with his gloved hands, looked her in the eyes, and began to talk with her in a comforting voice. "Honey, please don't do this to yourself," he said.

My heart sank when I realized that Henry knew the woman. The compassion he was displaying caused me to get emotional. The woman looked up at Henry with tears in her eyes. I could see her pain. I could also see her appreciation for the empathy another human being was showing her at the most difficult moment of her life. Back at the firehouse, I asked Henry who she was. I did not expect his response to be, "I don't know, but she's someone daughter."

I learned a huge lesson from my brother Henry on that day. We should all treat people we are helping as if they are our mothers, fathers, grand-parents, or children. To expand on that, we should treat the structure as if it is our own home. We should treat people's personal possessions as if they are our own. That's what leaders do. If you can develop that kind of atmosphere and attitude, everything else falls into place. It's called compassion. It's called empathy. It's called serving others.

Corporations wish they could duplicate the respect from the public that firefighters have. If we lose that respect, it's *our* fault. When my sister's house burned down on New Year's Eve, the Lafayette Fire Department took up a collection to replace my niece's toys. Why? Empathy. After 9/11, thousands of fire departments throughout the country took up collections and raised money for the victims' families. Why? Empathy.

Empathy is being aware of what is happening in others' lives. Perhaps this story will illustrate the point. A woman is sitting on the subway in NYC. She is reading a book when a man enters the train with his three young children, all under the age of 4. The man sits down as the train pulls away. Within minutes, the kids begin horsing around and playing. They become loud, distracting the woman and others on the train. She looks over at the man with a scowl, but he is just sitting there, oblivious to the commotion his kids are causing. Unable to take it anymore, the woman barks, "Sir, are you going to just sit there, or are you going to control your children?"

The man looks at her and says, "I'm so sorry." After a moment, he adds, "Their mother passed away last week. This is the first time they have played since it happened. I didn't have the heart to ask them to stop."

I'm sure that story hit some kind of nerve with you. It should—after all, we are all only human. When compassion is removed from a person, there's not much left. Of course, that's just my opinion. You may or may not agree, but today's fire service leaders are more than just tactical strategists. They are also marriage counselors, therapists, and advisers. The week I was writing this section, I received calls from four members of my group who were facing personal challenges. One was dealing with a recent separation, one was facing a possible medical leave he wasn't prepared for, one's wife was diagnosed with a serious illness, and another's promotion was postponed for the second time. They were all dealing with personal challenges and each needed advice and an ear. Sometimes calls like this come to me while I am off duty, sometimes when I'm on duty. Either way, I am grateful that these individuals felt comfortable enough to share their challenges with me. What type of person would I have been if I said, "Okay, but get back to work . . ." without showing them that I was empathetic to their challenge?

I don't know if I gave them the right advice. Many times all I do is listen and remind them that we have free counseling through the employee's assistance program through our town. One of the things I do is simply remind them that we all have challenges. I'm a believer that we are all currently in a crisis, just coming out of a crisis, or heading toward a crisis. Some may say that's a pessimistic viewpoint, but I'm far from pessimistic. I just know that when people feel isolated and alone, they need to know others have gone through it and come out okay.

In short, consider this. What most people want in a leader is something that's very difficult to find: they want someone who listens. Be that person.

....

"I believe empathy is the most essential quality of civilization."

—*Roger Ebert*

....

Summary

It's been said, "Firefighters are constantly meeting new people and spending the worst moments of their lives with them." Don't lose sight of that fact. As firefighters, our job isn't just to put the fire out, it's also to provide guidance for the people we serve and protect. Showing empathy means being kind and tactful when dealing with people who have just lost property, valuables, or worse—loved ones.

Suggestions for improvement

Treat others the way you would like to be treated.

Assertive

Assertiveness is a core communication skill. Being assertive means that you express yourself effectively and stand up for your point of view while also respecting the rights and beliefs of others. In corporate America they talk about boosting your self-esteem, earning the respect of others, and learning how to say no through assertiveness. Those are all valid points, but in the fire service, if orders are not followed, someone can be seriously injured or worse. It's about more than just being confident and direct in putting forward your views, it's about being firm.

Assertiveness on the fireground is in line with assertiveness on the battlefield, where orders are given and must be followed. The exception is when safety is compromised and performing a requested task would unduly endanger the lives of civilians or firefighters. Remember the risk analysis we spoke about in the Determination section? We risk a lot to save savable lives, we risk little to save savable property, and we risk nothing to save lives and property already lost.

As a leader in any profession, you cannot be assertive without having posture. I'm not talking about body language. I'm talking about the way you come across. In Ryan Chamberlin's book *Now You Know*, he describes *posture* this way: "If there were ever a concept universal to success in creating first—and lasting—impressions, it would be the concept of posture. Posture works in every area of life. When you were a child, you were told that you needed good posture, but that advice was in reference to how you were sitting or standing. This is a different type of posture. With regard to personal development, *posture is the way people receive you*. Posture is ultimately the summation of several character qualities, such as your attitude, belief systems, commitment, and self-image. There are, however, certain principles that, when learned, can have a dramatic effect on how people feel about you and what you say. When you remain in control of the situation and prevent others from taking control away from you, you send subliminal signals of competence, confidence, success, and a multitude of other positive impressions. The challenge with posture is that it cannot be faked."

At the fireground command level, true posture is described with two words—*command presence*. An incident commander who is in control of a situation, who gives precise instructions and makes proactive decisions, has command presence.

Being assertive does not mean you have to yell to get your point across. You can, and should, do everything in your power to remain calm in all situations, even if you feel that you are losing control (fig. 2–17). The way you react at a car fire should be similar, if not the same, as the way you react at a high-rise fire. Your job is not just to get others to move in the direction you want them to move. It's to *inspire* others to take action. Assertive communication is based on mutual respect. It's an effective communication style. Being assertive is a way of showing others that you respect yourself, because you're willing to stand firm in your beliefs.

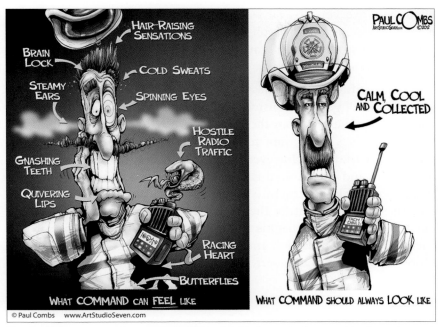

Fig. 2–17. As command, you must always appear in control, no matter how stressed out you really are.

Of course, it's not just what you say—your message—but also how you say it that's important. Being assertive, when done correctly, is a great way to deliver your message. If you communicate in a way that's too passive or too aggressive, your message may get lost because people are too busy reacting to your delivery.

Some people seem to be naturally assertive, but if you're not one of them, you can learn to be more assertive. It starts by being conscious of your body language. When a person is nervous, he or she subconsciously groups together gestures that make him or her easy to read. These are called gesture clusters, and I cover them in the next chapter under communication and presentations. To give a few quick examples, here is how gesture clusters work. Raising your eyebrows, biting your lower lip, and fidgeting around tells a person you are not confident in your ability. Square shoulders, chin up, and eye contact sends the completely opposite message. Speaking in a clear and confident manner will also help you come across as an assertive person. Be sure to speak loudly enough for everyone to hear you. Be decisive. People will respond better if they know exactly what you want out of them. Don't allow yourself to get easily frustrated, and if you do become frustrated, address the issue head on. Know when to say *go* and when to say *no*, and say it firmly.

Don't confuse assertiveness with aggressiveness. Firefighters don't like the idea of going defensive (pulling companies out of the building and fighting the fire from the outside). They often confuse this with strategic failure. They want to be in the building, taking the fire on, doing what they do. However, if you are in a leadership role on the fireground, and you see an unsafe practice, say something. If you are the IC and you think the structure is severely compromised, pull firefighters out. In the heat of battle, they may disagree with your call, but the moment that building begins to fall apart, you will become their best friend, a competent leader, and the smartest person on the fireground. More importantly, your assertiveness may have saved lives (fig. 2–18).

Fig. 2–18. Firefighters don't like taking a defensive stance, but a strong leader will not hesitate to order them out if the scene is unsafe.

Assertive leaders make decisions, communicate their decisions, and give direction. They do not think about doing something, they simply step up and do it.

....

"Assertive leaders express themselves effectively and stand up for their point of view, while also respecting the rights and beliefs of others."

....

Summary

To be assertive is to be aggressively self-assured and strong in your convictions without violating the rights of others. Assertive firefighters are confident. They know what to do on the fireground (and around the firehouse), and they know how to do it. More importantly, they don't need to be told to do it. They just do it, and when they recognize an unsafe practice, they are confident enough to stop the act before someone gets hurt.

Suggestions for improvement

Develop a values and belief system that allows you to assert yourself. Take a moment to think about your options, then be self-assured when you make a decision. You should be firm, but not overly aggressive. It is always wise to remember the third trait of a strong fire service leader is adaptability, so you can quickly adjust your strategy when necessary.

Courageous

Twenty seconds of courage can alter your entire life. Think about it. I did it when I approached a stunningly beautiful girl at Jenks in Pt. Pleasant Beach years ago, even though my friends said I didn't stand a chance. There was plenty to be nervous about, but that girl became my wife and today we have an amazing life together and three beautiful children. It all started with 20 seconds of courage . . . followed by a bit of nervous, incoherent babbling on my part.

Have you ever seen the photo of FDNY's Mike Kehoe making his way up the stairwell of the World Trade Center on 9/11 as civilians are lined up, trying to get down? That photo has been seen by millions of people. The picture tells a story. When you look at Kehoe's face, you can't help but to notice that he looks a little nervous. Wouldn't you have been? Whatever is going on in his mind, he is obviously pressing forward, toward the unknown. That photo serves as a constant reminder that courage isn't the absence of fear. It's the management of fear.

Everyone knows firefighters run toward danger while everyone else is running away. I could write this entire section on the fact that firefighting is one of the most courageous professions in the world. We can pat each other on the back and say, "Yeah, we're brave!" and be done with it. That may make the firefighters who read this book feel good for about three seconds, but if I were to write all the reasons why a person who wears bunker gear is perceived as being courageous, I'd be wasting your time and mine. Instead, let's take it one step further.

Are you really willing to put it all on the line? At some point in your career, every firefighter will encounter an invisible wall. The wall is symbolic. It is the one people must burst through when they are not sure they can push further than they already have. No one knows what they are truly capable of until that moment happens (fig. 2–19). What makes firefighters courageous, in my eyes, isn't what they do day in and day out, it's what they are *willing* to do. Thucydides, the ancient Greek historian, said it better than I can: "The bravest are surely those who have the clearest vision of what is before them, glory and danger alike, and yet notwithstanding, go out and meet it."

Fig. 2–19. Firefighters never know when they are going to have to push through the symbolic brick wall.

Unlike the past, the fire service, like most of corporate America, had to shift its thinking since tough economic times befell us in 2008. It takes a different type of courage to be a leader in our field today. With the constant threat of restructuring, layoffs, demotions, staffing reductions, and closings of companies and fire stations, someone has to *step up and lead*. It takes courage to stand up and voice your opposition to the governing body of your municipality. We all know most politicians are professional debaters (I'm being kind with my choice of words). And no one can argue the fact that a public sparring with a politician is never fun for a municipal employee. But someone has to meet with the powers that be and say what needs to be said in order to preserve a sufficient level of efficiency. They may cry about funding being scarce, but someone needs to point out the fact that if a fire department is understaffed, the entire community suffers. The people who live and work in that community cannot expect to receive the same level of service they have become accustomed to if the fire department suffers a 20% reduction in staff. Too many politicians use "mutual aid" as a Band-Aid. They need to be educated on the rapid progress of fire within a dwelling or the golden hour of survival at a vehicle accident. They need to understand that an additional 20 minutes added to a response time of second alarm units can be the difference between success and failure, and life and death.

It takes courage to lead a movement of public education. It takes even more courage to lead a movement to educate politicians. If you find yourself in a position where you have to speak to those who are threatening to make the types of changes we just mentioned, remember this simple guide: (1) get the facts, (2) prepare, and (3) present. The more prepared you are, the better your chances are of getting your point across in a professional and educated manner.

I should also mention three other types of courage that will serve you well: moral courage, physical courage, and courageous communication.

- Moral courage means having the inner strength to stand up for what is right and to accept blame when something is your fault.

- Physical courage means that you can continue to function effectively when there is physical danger present (fig. 2–20).

- Courageous communication means that you are willing to have the hard conversations that are necessary to lead during difficult circumstances. To communicate courageously means you never allow the way you would like things to be color the way things actually are.

Leadership requires the courage to make hard decision (and not just on the fireground). Jim Rohn said, "You cannot make progress without making decisions." Leadership isn't about taking a poll and picking the best option for everybody. You may lose fans when you make hard decisions, but you lose respect if you make decisions based on what's popular instead of what's right.

Fig. 2–20. Firefighters need physical courage, which means they must function at a high level under dangerous and difficult circumstances.

Hernando Cortez was a Spanish conquistador who, in 1519, assembled an army of 500 and set out to take the world's richest treasure that had been held by the Aztec Empire for 600 years. Army after army had tried to take this treasure, but they all failed because the natives outnumbered and outfought them. Cortez knew what he was up against, and he knew the natural instinct of his army. He knew that when they landed on Veracruz they would be tired and hungry. He also knew they would realize, for the first time, they were severely outnumbered and outmatched. Cortez believed his army would try to retreat to the boats. He needed to make their level of commitment beyond that of the others who had tried before him. When they reached their destination, Cortez gathered his army on the day of the battle. I'm sure they expected a strategic talk, maybe a motivational speech, but Cortez knew that would not be enough. Instead he turned to men with torches and said three words: "Burn the boats." As a result of that commitment, Cortez and his army defeated and conquered the Aztec Empire, and they took the treasure. Cortez knew that life shrinks or expands in proportion to one's courage. Because he understood this, he was able to make a hard decision that enabled his army to accomplish what no other had been able to.

That story reminds me of the saying: big goals require big commitments, and big commitments require courage.

....

"One man with courage is a majority."

—*Thomas Jefferson*

....

Summary

The first words that come to most people's minds when they think of firefighters are *courageous* and *brave*. Courage is what allows you to remain calm while recognizing fear. Moral courage means having the inner strength to stand up for what is right and to accept blame when something is your fault. Physical courage means that you can continue to function effectively when there is physical danger present. Courageous communication means that you are willing to have the hard conversations that are necessary to lead during difficult circumstances.

Suggestions for improvement

You can begin to control fear by practicing self-discipline and calmness. If you fear doing certain things that are required in your daily life, force yourself to do them until you can control your reaction. Lead by example. It doesn't take a hero to order someone into battle; it takes a hero to lead others into battle from the front line. Last, keep in mind, courage isn't the absence of fear; it's the management of fear.

Honorable

The honorable leader often stands alone—at least, for a short while. This is mainly because the path of the honorable leader is a difficult one. It's the parent who puts children before career, the person who stands up against a crowd, the worker who doesn't swear or cuss when everyone else around him does.

The fire service is one of the few professions that is rich with tradition and honor. The day a firefighter takes the oath is a special one. The individual is usually surrounded by family members and congratulated with the applause of the crowd. The same can be said of a promotional ceremony. My wife stood by my side, and my son Thomas held the Bible as I was sworn in (fig. 2–21). My parents, friends, family members, and coworkers were there, and we all went to out to celebrate after. Members wear their dress uniforms to events like parades, formal gatherings, and funerals. They wear their badges and citation bars with pride. In my town, we even have a historic firehouse that has been converted into an event hall where firefighter unions meet and parties are held. The walls are covered with memorabilia—old helmets, photos of previous firefighter-of-the-year recipients, and photos of fires, our members and their families. Why? Because we believe in honor.

Fig. 2–21. The fire service is rich with tradition and honor. This photo was taken at my promotional ceremony.

The brotherhood we preach about is honorable. It's more than just a word or a bumper sticker on your car. When Hurricane Floyd hit New Jersey, my house was one of many that were destroyed. At the time, I was living in Little Falls. The area was known for flooding, but my street was not. I spent the day working. We responded to more than five calls an hour during the heart of the storm—car accidents, downed primary wires, flooded streets, roofs, and basements. At 6:00, I left work to go home. My normal 25-minute commute took more than 2 hours due to the flooded roads and highways. When I arrived at my exit, I was shocked to see the river flowing down my street. I had to sleep in a shelter that night. The next morning, I was able to make it down my street to discover $5\frac{1}{2}$ feet of water in my house. It was a bi-level, and the entire first floor was destroyed. I was devastated. There are only a few things I remember vividly about that event. One of those things was the feeling I had when several trucks full of firefighters showed up at my house, unexpectedly, to help me gut and replace the walls. It was brotherhood . . . it was honor. It's what sets firefighters apart from any other group of people I have ever known.

By default, a firefighter is considered honorable in the public's eye the day he or she puts on a uniform, because the fire service, as an overall organization, has earned that reputation. But it only takes one slip-up to destroy a reputation. Each and every one of us must work to preserve this valuable trait. The only way to preserve honor is to be honorable. Are you an honorable leader? Honorable leaders see, with great clarity, the path to a better life for all. They lead by example. They live a life of integrity. They don't start rumors; they stop them. They accept responsibility. They understand that, although it is easy for human beings to dodge responsibilities, we cannot dodge the consequences of dodging our responsibilities. Honorable leaders also take ownership. Whatever the outcome, they assume responsibility.

Strong leadership is based on character. Your character is built on honor and integrity. I had the privilege of sitting in the Georgia Dome, along with 20,000 other people, and listening to General Norman Schwarzkopf give a talk about leadership. He was discussing some of the principles that helped him with the Gulf War. He gave a bulleted list of points, and I took several pages of detailed notes, but he ended by saying this. "If you happen to forget all that, just remember these two things and they will serve you well." Of course, I stopped writing and focused on the two things he was about to say. He said, "If you want to be an effective leader, you must always (1) take charge and (2) do the right thing." Ironically, I lost those notes in the flood. I forgot the bulleted list of leadership principles, but I never forgot those two things.

Honor is not a trait you can possess only during the times you are on duty. True honor is a 24/7/365 gig. You are just as honorable at a structure fire as you are at the local bar watching a playoff game. On that note, here's a bit of advice. Place emphasis on your values and stay honorable to God, your family, and your job. Surround yourself with ethical people. If you are part of the selection committee for new hires, screen them carefully. Tell them what you expect before they arrive to work on their first day: We don't steal, lie, fight, or betray our brotherhood. We don't vent our frustrations in public or on social media sites. I speak to high school kids on career day about the profession of firefighting. Although I spend the majority of my time telling them what a firefighter does and how to become one, one of the things I talk about with them is the same thing I often talk about with new firefighters. I'd like to share it with you right now. One radical or off-color post on a social media site can make people see you in an entirely different light. It takes a lifetime to build a good reputation, and if you are not careful, only seconds to destroy it.

....

"No person was ever honored for what he received.
Honor has been the reward for what he gave."

—*Calvin Coolidge*

....

Summary

To be honorable means you are worthy of honor and high respect. This is a by-product of the other traits listed in this chapter. When you put honesty, integrity, sense of duty, and sound moral principles above all else, you are operating in an honorable and ethical way.

Suggestions for Improvement

Be absolutely honest and truthful at all times. Stand up for what you believe is right. Always do the right thing. If it doesn't feel right, it probably isn't. If it is not legal, moral, or ethical, don't do it!

Leaders Teach

If you look at the first letters of each of the 12 previous traits, you will find that they spell the 13th, and perhaps the most important, trait: Leaders Teach! Think about this for a moment: If you possessed the combined knowledge of 100 competent firefighters who are great at what they do, you'd still have a lot to learn about our job.

Of course, you'd also be great at what you do, but the fact is, the list of areas we must specialize in is never-ending. Firefighting, hazardous material response, and technical rescue operations sound like a nice little package, but it would take a years of training to truly master any one of those three areas. And that's just the tip of the iceberg, as they say; what about emergency medical treatment, fire prevention and awareness, and officer development for up-and-coming leaders in the fire service? I am putting it all in general categories, but I'm sure you get the point. It's important to recognize that we all have strengths and weaknesses, which is why we need to share knowledge with others.

When talking about training probies, my brother once said, "A senior firefighter who doesn't share his knowledge with others is no more valuable than a door chock." He is 100% right. Your duty as a firefighter—and especially as a leader—is to pass your knowledge and experience on to new members (fig. 2–22).

Fig. 2–22. Firefighters have a responsibility to share their knowledge with others.

One of the first things I do with new firefighters is hand them a copy of an article I had written with Deputy Chief Mike Terpak titled "25 Things Every Probationary Firefighter Should Know and Do." The article gives them tips that I wish someone shared with me when I first joined the fire service. I know these individuals are going to learn firefighting skills in the academy and on the training ground, but someone also has to tell them how to approach the job overall. We tried to help accomplish this by providing the following 25 points, which we cover in detail in the article.

1. Respect the job.

2. Arrive early.

3. Be social.

4. Respect and learn from a senior firefighter.

5. Be proactive around the firehouse.

6. Be the first to rise and the last to sleep.

7. Find a mentor.

8. Know your riding position and responsibilities.

9. Check your equipment daily.

10. Wear your safety gear.

11. Ask questions.

12. Talk to the off-going crew.

13. Lead by example.

14. Don't try to force acceptance.

15. Leave your ego at the door.

16. Respect your elders.

17. Stay physically fit.

18. Stay mentally fit.

19. If you feel stressed, tell your officer.

20. Have fun.

21. Be a team player.

22. Be accountable.

23. Respect the public.

24. Make safety your priority.

25. Pay it forward. (Teach others what you have learned.)

I've seen far too many new firefighters come into the firehouse and try to fit in too quickly. This usually creates a mess. Those of you who have dealt with a similar situation know exactly what I am referring to. I usually start by reminding the probie of what I call the golden rule, which is, "God gave you two ears and one mouth, use them proportionately." That, by the way, is advice for us all. I elaborate by saying, "I remind myself every day that I will not learn anything by talking. If I am going to learn anything, it's going to be by asking questions and listening. If I have to do this, you have to do it also."

When I have new firefighters assigned to my shift, I sit them down and explain why they should check their tools every morning, before breakfast, as Kevin Becker does, as explained in the Loyalty section. It's essential that we teach about the importance of taking care of the three Fs: firefighters, fire apparatus, and fire stations.

That's a good start when dealing with probationary firefighters, but what about officers? As a chief officer, I want my captains to be competent enough to do my job in my absence. My goal has always been to help inspire layered leadership.

Layered Leadership is a fancy way of saying that 99% of all leadership occurs not from the top but from the middle of an organization. This occurs when you take time to help develop people who work with you. This also plays back into the concept of Lane Theory that I mentioned in the Selfless section. When you teach, you will also discover what a person's strengths are. A fire service leader must know where, when, and how to use the talents, skills, and abilities of each of his or her team members. That is best way to ensure the overall success of your team.

Don't believe your own press! Too many people reach a level of success and think they can sit back in their new position and—for lack of a better word—coast. Don't let this be you. Just because you teach doesn't mean you are finished learning. I had written this book to teach what I know about leadership, but I've read hundreds of books on the topic of leadership—I've used and fine-tuned these theories, tips, and techniques both in and out of the fire service. I've developed, tested, and revised my own theories and techniques, and I'm still learning every day. By the time you read these pages, I'm sure some of the information in this book will have evolved. We are constantly learning, growing, and changing. Your job is to help others realize that fact.

"Expectations" is a key word when it comes to teaching, for two reasons: (1) It's important to remember that people will rise or fall to meet your expectations of them, and (2) you have to set your expectations up front. It's difficult to get on someone when you didn't give him or her a game plan first.

Teaching tips

1. The four-step process. I cannot provide you with the one best way to teach everyone, mainly because everyone is different. To be able to get through to 20 men and women with 20 different personalities is not an easy task. It takes awareness and skill. The one thing I can tell you is that, when it comes to learning tasks, it's been proven that the majority of us respond to a four-step learning process. As an instructor, try the following format (fig. 2–23):

1. You do it, they watch.

2. You do it along with them.

3. They do it, you watch.

4. You let them do the task alone.

Fig. 2–23. Kearny Firefighter Mike Richardson shares his knowledge of roof ventilation with probationary firefighters.

2. KISS. Another bit of advice I'd like to give you can be summed up by the acronym KISS, which stands for: Keep It Simple, Stupid. I certainly don't mean to call you stupid. I actually use that acronym to remind myself that many people have a tendency to overcomplicate a simple task. I don't want to be one of those people. When teaching, begin by stating the objective of the training, then end with a summary of what was learned.

3. Stories. I learned a long time ago that most of us learn more from a story. I can talk to a firefighter about the importance of wearing personal protective gear, or I can tell that individual the story about how my friend Ron spent 12 days in the burn center because of severe damage to his neck and ears after he forgot to put on his protective hood before entering a structure fire. Stories help capture people's attention and illustrate the point. Howard Gardner said, "Stories are the single most powerful tool in a leader's toolkit."

4. Be a mentor. If you don't have a formal mentoring program, that doesn't mean you can't be a mentor or assign one to a new firefighter. On that topic, you'd also be wise to choose your own mentor. Any wise person knows there is always someone wiser. When you are around wise people, remember that golden rule, "God gave you two ears and one mouth, use them proportionately." In chapter three I provide some tips on mentoring and mentorship programs.

I'll say this about teaching others. There is an abundance of opportunities to teach. Firefighters are great at passing on information. I'm always looking to pass on knowledge to others. When I go on a false alarm, even at 2:30 a.m., I'll take a few minutes before we return to quarters to point out something to a newer firefighter, such as a brick veneer or parapet wall, a dangerous fire escape, or the difference between blue, red, and yellow flames in relation to carbon monoxide. Even if no one ever did this for you, be the one who starts the tradition of doing it for others.

The ultimate goal of a leader is not just to teach, it's to inspire others. I love the quote by Eleanor Roosevelt: "A good leader inspires people to have confidence in the leader. A great leader inspires people to have confidence in themselves." This is best done by developing relationships. It's good to demand a lot from others around you, but only if you demand more from yourself.

When you find—or help develop—other leaders, don't make the mistake so many others do and micromanage them. The best way to manage leaders is to support them and let them run in their lane. In his book *Tribes, We Need You to Lead Us*, Seth Godin says this about finding leaders: "Find leaders (the heretics who are doing things differently and making change), and then amplify their work, give them a platform, and help them find followers. I hope that's not so simple that it gets ignored."

It is simple, but it works. It might be the most important practical idea in his entire book. It all falls in line with something called succession planning. True succession planning is an ongoing process that is designed to ensure the continued effectiveness of an organization at all levels. It can only be accomplished by training and developing new leaders to take over when positions become vacant. I remember reading an article about the city of San Antonio's first fire chief to come from outside the department. In the article, the interviewer asked the chief to clarify his statement about this being the last time a fire chief comes from the outside. He answered by saying "If there are not multiple qualified candidates who are capable of being the next San Antonio fire chief, then I have failed in one of my areas of focus. It would be very disappointing." Well said, Chief!

....

"A good leader inspires people

to have confidence in the leader.

A great leader inspires people

to have confidence in themselves."

—*Eleanor Roosevelt*

....

Leadership traits summary

Because it is important to always remember these essential leadership traits, use the acronym LEADERS TEACH. Each letter in the acronym corresponds to the first letter of one of the traits. By remembering this acronym, you will be better able to recall the traits. The beauty of this acronym is that it actually spells the 13th trait of a good fire service leader.

There are obviously other important traits for leaders, such as transparency, humility, good judgment, and strong motivational skills, but these 13 are vital to your success as a leader in the fire service. Your skill at exhibiting these qualities will be firmly linked with people's desire to follow your lead. Exhibiting the traits previously mentioned will inspire confidence in your leadership ability. Not exhibiting these traits or exhibiting the opposite of these traits will decrease your leadership influence with those around you, resulting in failure.

Leadership Failure

It would be a terrible mistake to end this section without covering some of the traits associated with failure. As important as it is to understand what makes a good leader, it's equally as important to understand why so many fail in leadership positions. Here is a quick list of some traits associated with poor leadership.

- Lack of passion
- Unclear vision
- Poor communication skills
- Avoiding taking risks
- Callousness
- Unethical behavior
- Poor self-management
- Incompetence
- Playing the victim
- Tearing others down
- Micromanaging
- First to take the credit
- Last to take the blame

When someone in a position of authority displays poor leadership traits, the mission he or she is trying to accomplish is doomed to fail. A fire service officer will never earn the respect of his or her crew without developing the qualities that align with those of great leaders. This is true in any profession.

Many of us have had an experience, at one time or another, of working under a person with poor leadership skills. My advice is this: pay attention to what that person is doing ineffectively, and then do the opposite.

Legacy of a Leader

When others who are under your leadership look at an action you have taken and think, "That just goes to show why you are the one in charge," you are on the right track. If these moments are infrequent, it is likely that some demonstrations of competency will help boost your leadership influence. By consciously making an effort to develop and exhibit the traits listed in this book, people will be more likely and willing to follow you. By exhibiting these traits on a regular basis, you will earn the respect of others and increase your effectiveness as an influential leader.

The actions you take daily may often seem insignificant, but if you repeat the correct actions every day, you will become a product of that repetitive action. Again, I'm talking again about the compound effect. For example, if you eat a candy bar every day, it may not seem like it's much, but if you ate a candy bar every day for five years, you would have eaten 1,825 of them—and your body would be affected by it. Replace that candy bar with an apple. One day, no big deal, but 1,825 apples later . . . you get the point. The compound effect will be a healthier you. The same can be said about your leadership actions. Proper actions, repeated daily, produce amazing long-term results.

You may have not thought about this, but you are creating your own legacy. Although that can be an overwhelming thought, it shouldn't be. The key is to develop the habits of a leader and take small steps every day. A friend of mine once sent me an e-mail that read as follows:

I am your constant companion.

I am your greatest helper or heaviest burden.

I will push you onward or drag you down to failure.

I am completely at your command.

Half of the things you do you might as well turn over to me and I will do them—quickly and correctly.

I am easily managed—you must be firm with me.

Show me exactly how you want something done and after a few lessons, I will do it automatically.

I am the servant of great people, and alas, of all failures as well.

Those who are great, I have made great. Those who are failures, I have made failures.

I am not a machine though I work with the precision of a machine plus the intelligence of a person.

You may run me for profit or run me for ruin—it makes no difference to me.

Take me, train me, be firm with me, and I will place the world at your feet.

Be easy with me and I will destroy you.

Who am I? . . . I am Habit.

If you develop the right habits and love your job; if you are loyal and eager to learn; if you adapt easily and are determined to get the job done no matter what, if you are enthusiastic, reliable, and selfless; if you are tough but empathetic; if you are assertive and courageous; if you are honorable and share your knowledge with others . . . you are ready to *step up and lead!*

3

LEADERSHIP SKILLS

Have you ever wondered how to get the best performance out of other people? Why do some people in leadership positions seem to have the respect of everyone around them, while others wonder why everyone leaves the room when they enter it? The most likely answer is that the first leader has skills with (and respect for) people, while the other does not.

Any firefighter will agree that he or she is more loyal to an officer who shows respect. The same can be true in any profession. Strategy and tactics are not only words that can be used when leading people on the fireground. The right strategy and tactics are also needed when managing change, delegating tasks, critiquing others, motivating a team, and dealing with insubordination.

Developing these types of skills will require work on your part. When you show that you are willing to put forth an effort, people take notice and things begin to change for the better. In today's world, leaders are needed at all levels. Even though the chief (or department head) may run the show and create the overall culture of a fire service organization, when leadership qualities can be found in people at all ranks, a subculture can be created that can supersede one that is created by one person. This can be a good or bad thing. As a deputy chief, I have witnessed and brought attention to good examples of leadership that have come from members of all ranks and positions. However, as easy as it is to identify good examples, it's just as easy to recognize bad ones.

I once asked a senior firefighter (I'll call him Phil) to train another, younger firefighter to drive and operate the tower ladder. After a couple weeks, I asked Phil how it was going, and he responded, "Not good. He can't do it."

"What do you mean, 'he can't do it'?" I asked.

"He isn't made for it," Phil elaborated. "He's *untrainable*."

Apart from the fact that *untrainable* is my least favorite word when it comes to building a successful team, I couldn't help but to wonder why Phil was saying this about a firefighter who seemed perfectly competent in my eyes. I met with the firefighter to talk with him about his lack of progress, and he assured me he could do the job. He felt he just needed "another day or two" to practice. I relayed this to Phil, who proceeded to stress his opinion, "He can't do it, Chief."

My immediate thought was that Phil was lazy and unwilling. A few weeks later, the firefighter was transferred to another group, which had nothing to do with Phil's assessment. The other group happened to be riding short due to retirements, and I had an extra firefighter. I sent him because he was the junior firefighter on my shift—a common practice in our industry. Within a week, the firefighter was driving the apparatus without any problems. It was obvious to me early on—and the transfer confirmed the fact—that Phil was the problem. He simply didn't want to take time to work with the firefighter. He didn't want to step up. From that moment on, I knew Phil was not a leader; although I really knew it long before that incident. The fact is Phil was the one who was unwilling to take the time to properly train this new firefighter, which is something I will elaborate on in the 3U section of this chapter. Although I discussed this incident with Phil and dealt with it appropriately, I often look back and wonder if I should have transferred him instead.

Exhibiting the leadership traits we discussed in the chapter 2 is a great start, but leadership—the act—is a skill, and like any skill it needs to be developed. This chapter introduces a number of skills that a fire service leader must possess. The right skill set will enable a leader to create the right culture—a culture of execution.

Talents, Skills, and Abilities

Take a moment to contemplate those three words—talents, skills, and abilities. Everybody has them. What are yours? What are you good at? Do you feel your talents, skills, and abilities are being utilized correctly?

If you work for someone else, there is a good possibility that you would answer no to that question. Why is that? Because most people in leadership positions never take the time to get to know what the people around them are good at. Now, let's flip the script. Are you currently leading a team? Are you guilty of making this same mistake?

Many people in leadership positions fall into the trap of thinking they need to constantly try to prove that they know more than everyone else. This is a big mistake, and I'd like to present you with a different way of looking at things. If you have more talent, skills, and abilities than everyone on your team combined, you have a weak team.

Smart leaders will not only want smarter and more talented people on their team, they will actively seek them out. "Positional leaders" (those simply with a title, rank, or position of authority), on the other hand, tend to become threatened by talented people. Someone outperforming them, or getting the credit for a specific job, is a blow to their ego and self-esteem (fig. 3–1). Because of this, they tend to, consciously or unconsciously, sabotage the efforts of others in an effort to keep from appearing weak.

Fig. 3–1. Don't let your ego get so big it becomes an issue.

To become a true leader, you should avoid making this mistake. Instead, find out what skills each of your team members brings to the table, and play to those strengths. Give team members responsibility and look for ways to help them shine and utilize their skills.

Every person around you is unique and has a distinct skill set, but you have to take time to get to know who does what. Make sure you are utilizing those talents correctly. Imagine coaching a high school football team and taking the kid with the best arm and leadership skills and making him your place kicker. It doesn't make any sense. Many organizations are guilty of making that same mistake.

In the fire service we have discovered that some people are made for engine company duties while others are more equipped for the type of work ladder company personnel do (figs. 3–2 and 3–3). Both require a different attitude and skill set. Even on each apparatus, there will be three or four individuals with different talents, skills, and abilities. One may be great with medical emergencies, while another is an expert at forcible entry. A true leader will know the talents of his or her team members and utilize them without trying to take all the credit.

I know of chief officers who are guilty of making this mistake time and time again. They have talented writers, but asked poor writers to craft public relations articles. They have great instructors, but don't allow them to work on developing training evolutions. They have gifted networkers, but don't give them time to visit other departments to develop relationships that could benefit their organization with regard to sharing information or organizing mutual aid response agreements. They have knowledgeable firefighters with a variety of talents, but they don't even know it. Some say it's because they don't care. I think it goes deeper than that. I believe some of them actually think they are smarter and more talented than everyone else, and they aren't going to let anyone tell them otherwise. I am describing the classic micromanager who does not know how to utilize resources properly. This person is always angry because others don't know what he wants, but he never communicates with anyone until something goes wrong—then he blames everybody else for things going bad . . . everyone but himself. Do you know anyone like that? Earlier in my career, I remember discussing micromanagers with a talented friend who owns several successful companies.

Figs. 3–2 and 3–3. Engine and ladder company duties are different and therefore require different talents, skills, and abilities from the individuals operating on each apparatus.

"I used to work for a micromanager," he said.

"That must have been painful for a guy like you." I replied.

"It was, but I am grateful for the experience because watching his inability to lead people enabled me to identify what doesn't work, so I didn't make the same mistakes when I started my first business."

It's unfortunate to come across a fire department with an ineffective leader; however, throughout my career I have found that the majority of leaders within the fire service are smart enough to respect the talents, skills, and abilities of their members.

Here is a simple way to help you learn to value the diversity of your team members. Create a check sheet. On the top column, list all the talents, skills, and abilities you want and need on your team. Down the left side, put the names of your team members. As you learn about each one, place a check next to the categories he or she excels in.

....

Talents, skills, and abilities check sheet

Name	Effective communicator	Problem solver	Adapts easily	Aggressive on the fire-ground	Well organized	Educated
Mark	✓	✓		✓	✓	
Donna		✓	✓		✓	✓
Jeff	✓			✓		
Scott	✓		✓	✓		✓

....

Customize the list any way you want, but understand that as a team leader, a big part of your job is to identify the gifts that others around you have and utilize them.

Fireproof Tip

Know your team members' strengths (and weaknesses) and utilize their talents, skills, and abilities in a way that benefits the team as a whole. Only leaders with character, competence, and confidence are wise enough to want to be surrounded by those who are, in some ways, their superior. Those leaders tend to build very strong teams.

Delegation

A leader will accomplish far more through effective delegation than by taking on 100% of the responsibility of every project and/or making the terrible mistake of chronic micromanagement. Delegation is one of the most important aspects of time management. It's right up there with setting priorities and avoiding time-wasting activities. As a tour commander, I would have found it impossible to arrive on the scene of a three-alarm residential structure fire and try to manage the scene, secure the area, raise ladders to the second floor, advance hose lines, and treat the victims by myself (fig. 3–4). It would be ridiculous for one person to even consider taking on all those roles. So why, when it comes to administrative tasks, do so many people try to do just that? I've known many individuals in the private sector who have tried to "do it all," only to have their personal performance and physical health deteriorate because of the stress and unnecessary burden they've invited into their lives.

Dividing tasks multiplies your chances of success. Effective delegation is an absolute necessity when it comes to an organization's success. Subsequently, failure to delegate will ultimately result in failure to adequately develop your team. In the end, everyone will suffer. People need to feel the heat, pressure, and tension of tackling bigger tasks; otherwise, they will never be ready to take on more responsibility. If you don't develop your people and let them feel a little heat today, they'll end up getting burned when you need them the most. The best way to prevent this is through delegation.

Fig. 3–4. It's impossible for the IC to take on every role on the fireground, so why do so many leaders try to do just that when it comes to administrative tasks?

Knowing how to delegate (and who to delegate to) will not only make your overall job easier, it will also show the rest of your company that you are a strong leader who has faith in them, the result of which will be greater efficiency and increased morale across the board.

When leaders delegate responsibilities, they should give their team members the authority to take whatever actions necessary (legally, morally, and ethically, of course) to complete the task and achieve the desired end result. This holds just as true in corporate America as it does in the fire service. Once you assign a task, don't look over the shoulders of your subordinates and question why they are doing it this way rather than that way. Instead, make it a priority to arrange things so the task can be completed without interruptions, from you or anyone else, that may impede progress.

Don't be fooled into thinking that delegation is the simple act of passing the buck. As sure as there are rewards for proper delegation, there are absolute consequences for poor delegation. In order for supervisors to delegate effectively, they should first feel secure about their own position and understand the talents, skills, and abilities of those around them.

When a fire officer arrives first on the scene of a structure fire and establishes command, and four additional apparatus carrying 12 or more firefighters pull onto the scene shortly afterwards, the first thing those firefighters will do is radio, or walk up to the command post and ask the question, "What do you need?" Immediately, assignments are given, and off they go (fig. 3–5). One team will inevitably be assigned the job of searching the fire floor of the building, another will be sent in with a hose line with the task of confining the fire, and another will be assigned the job of ventilation. If the individuals leading these teams are well trained, you will not have to tell them how to do their assigned task; they'll already know how—and they should know how, because firefighters train every day just for that reason. As a chief officer, when I arrive on the fireground, I give out an assignment, knowing with 100% confidence that it is going to be completed within an acceptable time frame. I know this because I understand the abilities of each of my officers and firefighters. Being in this position takes the weight of the world off my shoulders.

Fig. 3–5. Delegation at the command level is easy when a leader knows the strengths of those around him.

The same way an incident commander delegates on the fireground is the way you should delegate tasks on an everyday basis. In our profession, this holds true whether we are assigning housework or tackling administrative projects, such as developing a fire prevention community awareness program. A smart officer will gather facts and accomplish specific tasks by effectively delegating those tasks to the appropriate firefighters. Delegation should happen in the planning, research, development, implementation, and evaluation stages of all projects, especially ones that are large and manpower intensive. The bottom line is that every job is easier when you delegate properly.

So, you like the idea of delegating, but you are so used to doing everything yourself that you don't know where to begin. Here are some tips on how to delegate effectively.

How to delegate

1. Establish and maintain an environment that is favorable to delegating.

This begins by creating team spirit. As a leader, you should clearly understand the task that you are delegating. If it is not clear in your own mind, you will not be able to communicate it to others. Take into consideration your expected result, the resources available to you, and the time frame in which the task needs to be accomplished.

Only when you fully understand what needs to be done will you be able to brief your team members thoroughly. When delegating assignments, be prepared to express the scope of the task, the desired results, the available resources, the sensitivity of the task, communication guidelines, deadlines, and of course your confidence in the person you select.

Once you have it all figured out, you're ready to delegate; however, don't lose sight of the fact that when you delegate, you are not relinquishing responsibility. As the leader, you are still in control of the overall project.

2. Select the right person for the job.

When I first took over my shift, I went around to each station, stood in front of the firefighters who worked there, and asked them to share a little about themselves, specifically, what skills they may have that could assist us on the fire scene or around the firehouse. We all learned things about each other that day. Some firefighters were licensed electricians or contractors; others had computer skills. One was a member of the state's urban search and rescue team. Having this knowledge made it easy for me to call on the right person for the right job.

When delegating, be sure the person understands that by accepting the assignment and accomplishing the task, both the team and the individual will benefit. A smart leader will be aware of the strengths and limitations of his or her team members and delegate accordingly. Ideally, the person chosen to tackle a task should have the talent, skills, ability, knowledge, enthusiasm, and time needed to get the job done. If you cannot find those qualities in one person, before selecting a delegate, ask questions like:

- Who is best equipped to handle this job?
- Who accepts challenges and is likely to rise to the occasion?
- Can one person do this job, or will it require multiple team members?
- Does the task require previous experience, or is training needed?
- Who would learn the most by accepting this responsibility?
- Who would benefit the least if assigned this task?
- Who can I trust to do the job?

3. Assure that the person accepting the assignment understands it (fig. 3–6).

When giving the assignment, encourage the delegate to ask questions in order to eliminate any confusion. Also be sure to express how much authority you are handing over. You may choose to provide guidance by saying something like, "Look into the problem, suggest a few possible solutions, and together we'll choose the best one." Or, you may have enough confidence in that individual to say, "Solve the problem and let me know when you're finished."

Be flexible, but set parameters and establish controls to ensure this authority and the accompanying power will be properly used. If necessary, inform other relevant team members of the situation. The person you are delegating the task to should not only have a clear picture of what you want, but should also be aware that by accepting the assignment, the delegate is taking a positive step forward in his or her own progress as a competent and valuable member of your organization.

Fig. 3–6. When delegating, be sure people understand the tasks you are assigning.

4. Keep an open door policy.

The lines of communication should always remain open. Make yourself available to provide assistance if and when needed. Let the delegate know he or she should make first contact, but ask that person to immediately inform you when things are not going according to plan.

If the task or project is one that will take several days, weeks, or even months to accomplish, schedule regular meetings just so you can acquire progress reports to make sure this project is moving forward, along with others that you may be working on. These meetings do not need to be more than a few minutes long. Your main focus is to find out what has been accomplished, what needs to be accomplished, and what problems, if any, have been encountered. (See the section on conducting effective meetings for more tips.)

5. Be prepared to accept and deal with the consequences of that person's actions if he or she does not meet your organization's expectations.

I believe it is essential that every one of the firefighters on my shift know I have his or her back if things unexpectedly go wrong. Your team needs to feel the same way. This does not mean that you have to accept less than their best effort. It simply means that when honest mistakes are made, you will approach the situation with a level head and take into consideration the fact that you assigned this task to this individual because you felt he or she was competent. An unsatisfactory outcome could be a result of situations that were out of the delegate's control. Since you delegated the assignment to a person you have confidence in, that individual absolutely deserves the benefit of the doubt.

6. Always reward performance.

Reward and recognition are vitally important when it comes to expressing appreciation. As I worked my way through the ranks, I've experienced and observed the reality that the people who voluntarily work the hardest are often those who feel the most appreciated. As a leader, it's your responsibility to show appreciation for a job well done by recognizing quality work privately and publicly. Never forget, it's not how much appreciation that you have for another person that's important. What's important is how much appreciation they feel. Sincere recognition will increase your effectiveness as a leader and keep team morale high. Don't reward hard-working team members by giving them more work than you give to others. Although that is a sign of respect for a competent individual, it is also poor management to put so much work on one person's shoulders that you fail to help develop the skills of others on the team. Consciously work to empower others in a way that they help you develop and execute your ideas and you will become a thousand times more efficient than you would by doing it yourself.

Fireproof Tip

The purpose of delegating is not to avoid work or unload difficult or tedious tasks to others. Effective delegation is an absolute necessity when it comes to a team's success. When you divide tasks, you multiply your chances of success. Failure to delegate will result in a failure to adequately develop your team. Through delegation, your team will grow in confidence; and they—and your entire organization—will benefit in the long run.

Dealing with Subordinate Problems (the 3U Method)

Ask any fire service leader if he or she has had problems with a subordinate, and you will likely receive a look that sarcastically implies, "Are you kidding me?"

It is inevitable, when a group of individuals with different personalities spend any significant amount of time together, that those personalities are going to clash and problems will surface. This is especially true in the fire service, where it is not uncommon for a group of individuals to spend 24 hours together. Put five different personalities together in a room for that long, and there are going to be challenges. Some may appear to be minor problems, such as the avoidance of daily housework duties or a sudden lack of interest in the job. Others are much more serious, such as refusing to obey orders around the firehouse, or worse, on the fireground. Minor problems are sometimes the by-product of a personal issue that has surfaced in the individual's life; however, whenever problems like this occur in the fire service, they must be immediately addressed by the subordinate firefighter's supervising officer (fig. 3–7). By doing so, we can begin to determine the reason for this change in behavior and identify any issues that can be resolved before they grow to become major problems, which will inevitably end up in the chief's office, or worse.

Fig. 3–7. When problems occur within the fire service, they should be immediately addressed. This will help ensure that individuals are ready to perform at a high level when the call comes in.

When you, as a leader, find yourself in a situation where you must step in to resolve a more serious issue, a private conversation between you and the individual may promptly escalate to the dreaded "meeting with the chief." If you thought being on the receiving end of the subordinate interview could be intimidating, just wait until you find yourself on the delivery end. After all, this isn't a mere job interview we're talking about. This is a legitimate problem that needs to be dealt with and corrected without delay; otherwise, it would have never made its way into your office.

This section will help guide you through the fact-finding process when interviewing a subordinate worker. Let's begin by defining the words *subordinate* and *insubordinate*.

sub·or·di·nate *adj.*

> 1. Belonging to a lower or inferior class or rank; secondary.
> 2. Subject to the authority or control of another.

in·sub·or·di·nate *adj.*

> Disobedient to authority

The subordinate interview

Organizational leaders in management positions must learn to deal with subordinate issues, such as conflict resolution or substandard performance. There is no shortage of information about how to conduct a formal subordinate interview and address serious problems, but I want to share the basics of conducting such an interview. I will preface this section by encouraging anyone in the fire service who has to take disciplinary action against an individual that goes beyond a written reprimand to consult with a governing body and/or seek legal advice before doing so.

Here are the basic components of a subordinate interview as it would occur within the fire service in a simple format.

1. **Gather facts.** Review all pertinent information (including the personnel files of all individuals who are involved or who witnessed the incident at hand; also review incident reports if necessary).

2. **Get it in writing.** Have those who are involved provide written reports of what occurred and why. This includes third-party witnesses.

3. **Schedule a meeting.** If you suspect that disciplinary action will be necessary, the individual(s) should be provided with the option of having union representation.

4. **Conduct the meeting**. Begin by putting the firefighter at ease. State the purpose of the meeting. Discuss positives about the individual before stating the problem at hand. When you do discuss the problem, use facts to support the reason this was brought to your attention, and explain why it's inappropriate behavior.

5. **Get the individual's side of the story.** Use open-ended questions to gather facts. Probe for answers and show empathy.

6. **Look for an underlying problem.** Don't discard the possibility that circumstances in the individual's personal life may be affecting his or her behavior, especially if behavior is uncharacteristic.

7. **Determine which of the 3Us you are dealing with (unaware, unable, or unwilling).** This is the main reason for the interview. The actions you take will be determined by which of the 3Us the individual falls under. I will cover the 3Us thoroughly in the next section.

8. **Discuss progressive discipline (1. verbal reprimand, 2. written reprimand, 3. suspension, 4. fines, and 5. termination).** Any time you take disciplinary action, you should explain what the next step may be if another issue arises.

9. **Develop a solution together and implement it.** You will achieve better results if the individual feels like he or she is playing an active role in determining what actions can be taken to correct the situation. When discussing solutions, take training (NFPA, organizational procedures, sensitivity training, specific training) and counseling (employee assistance programs, critical incident stress debriefing, etc.) into consideration.

10. **Summarize.** Recap the key points and the solution to ensure clarity.

11. **Set a follow-up meeting.** Stress that improvements need to be made within the specified time frame. Whenever appropriate, a strong leader will also ensure that what occurred in the meeting will remain confidential and that you have an open-door policy if the individual needs to discuss related issues.

12. **Inform the individual of the appeal process.** Discuss due process if the individual feels the actions taken to correct the situation are too harsh.

13. **Close on positive note.**

14. **Document and report.** Document in writing what occurred in the meeting and inform your superior of such.

15. **Monitor and evaluate the individual's progress until the next meeting.**

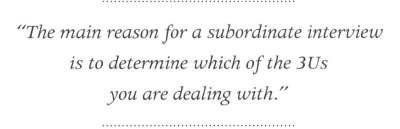

"The main reason for a subordinate interview

is to determine which of the 3Us

you are dealing with."

That is a brief overview of the subordinate interview process that is often followed in the fire service. As discussed in step 7, the main reason for the meeting is to determine which of the 3Us you are dealing with.

The 3Us

This section is about helping you ascertain whether the problem is serious.

The goal of a fact-finding interview is to determine what the problem is and attempt to develop a solution. This can only be accomplished after concluding if the individual is unaware, unable, or unwilling (otherwise known as the 3Us). If you fail to make this determination, whether informally or formally, you will not be able to take the appropriate corrective actions.

Here is a brief description of the 3Us:

- **Unaware.** Not aware or not conscious of what is going on.

- **Unable.** Lacking mental or physical capability or efficiency; incompetent.

- **Unwilling.** Boldly resisting authority or having a defiant attitude (insubordinate).

Consider it your job, as a leader, to determine if the individual is unaware that there is a problem, unable to fix it, or unwilling to fix it.

As you gather facts, you should begin contemplating your course of action. You can do this by thinking:

If he or she is *unaware*, I will . . .
If he or she is *unable*, I will . . .
If he or she is *unwilling*, I will . . .

After determining which category the subordinate falls into, implement the appropriate solution. As previously mentioned, within the fire service, the solution may include some form of training, counseling, and/or a variety of other possibilities, all depending on the issue(s) at hand. Here's an illustration of how to deal with each of the 3Us individually. Consider the following example.

A third-year firefighter has been displaying uncharacteristic behavior. He is considered to be an ambitious and enthusiastic firefighter; however, over the past few weeks he has been repeatedly showing up late for work, performing below standard, and complaining frequently about various issues in the firehouse and on the fireground. After receiving complaints from other firefighters, you bring the firefighter into your office to speak with him about the way he has been acting. You begin to ask the right questions and probe for answers.

Depending on the response(s) you receive, you should be able to determine which of the 3Us you are dealing with. *Note:* Although these are serious issues, this is an informal fact-finding interview, and the information you discover during this process may lead to a serious underlying problem that will require you to take firm and immediate action.

If he is *unaware* of his actions, perhaps the talk will be enough for him to take the appropriate corrective actions. You should still schedule some form of training, such as reviewing any related policies and procedures the individual may be violating. You should also discuss what you expect from the individual and have him acknowledge it, so there is no misunderstanding. The key word here is *awareness*. If the problem persists, you will no longer be dealing with a person who is unaware. You will now have to address the issue based on the understanding that the individual is either unable or unwilling to correct the situation. After a meeting of this nature, be sure to document the incident for your records.

If he is *unable* to change his actions, you have a more serious situation on your hands. This individual will be showing signs of incompetence. It is tough to generalize how to deal with this situation, but there are some basic steps you should begin taking. First, the actions outlined in the previous paragraph must be repeated to ensure the person is, in fact, aware of what is expected of him. If it becomes clear that he is unable to fix the problem(s), or if this is a repeat offense, you will have to make your superior(s) aware of the situation. Again, your organization's policies and procedures should be followed at this point, but be sure to document the actions you have taken so far. You may have to refer to your notes at a later date. Be sensitive to the possibility that the person may be dealing with a personal issue that is leading to his inability to function at an acceptable level. If this is the case, private counseling may be the answer. Either way, if this is a repeat offense, you should have the individual write a special report explaining what is happening.

If he is *unwilling* to change his actions, more drastic measures must be taken. In this scenario, it is assumed that you have already ruled out the possibility that the individual is *unaware* or *unable*. You are now dealing with someone who is boldly resisting authority or who has a defiant attitude. This person is insubordinate, and the situation must be immediately bumped up the chain of command. There may not be much you can do to a person who complains, but there are definite actions a department will have to take when a person consistently shows up late for work or otherwise performs below an acceptable standard. Once again, your organization's policies and procedures should be followed, and your actions should be documented. Your report, along with the special report completed by the individual, should be immediately sent to your superior.

Whenever you bring an individual into your office to address issues of concern, and it becomes obvious the individual is at fault, disciplinary action is necessary. Don't be fooled into thinking that this always mean you have to "drop a hammer." This simply means that the five steps of progressive discipline should be followed. They are, in order: verbal reprimand, written reprimand, suspension, fines, and termination.

If, in fact, the issue at hand requires more than "a talk" with the individual in question, the appropriate solution should be determined by the head of your organization and only after proper counsel.

Fireproof Tip

It's wrong to jump to the conclusion that an individual who has not had any problems in the past is deliberately doing something wrong. The right thing to do is conduct a subordinate interview to try and determine if the individual is unaware, unable, or unwilling. Then address the root of the problem properly.

Critiquing Others

As with any profession, there will be times when a firefighter will perform at an unacceptable level. This can occur in the firehouse or out in the public's eyes (which in many ways, is far worse). When these incidents are witnessed and/or brought to your attention, they must be addressed. The majority of the time, constructive criticism will be needed. Critiquing, when done correctly, falls under the same category as constructive criticism. Many times, critiquing the actions of an entire crew on the training ground will benefit an entire team. In this instance, it's wise to remember that you are simply trying to fine-tune the overall performance of the team (fig. 3–8). However; in order to skill-fully critique an individual, you should understand that, unlike praise, which has a greater effect when done in front of others, critiquing should be done privately. If it is a serious matter, firefighters sometimes want some form of support (such as a union representative or a senior firefighter) in the room. If that's the case, they are entitled to have all the support they want. Otherwise, the correct action to take is to meet with the individual one-on-one. After you choose a private setting, use the following proven format that is used both in the fire service as well as corporate America.

Fig. 3–8. Although constructively critiquing the performance of a crew on the training ground is an acceptable practice, singling out individuals should be done in a private setting.

Format for critiquing others

1. Begin on a positive. Remember, at this point you may not know if the individual is *unaware* of the problem, *unable* to correct the problem, or *unwilling* to correct the problem. You don't want to assume the worst. This person, most likely, has positive attributes. I always take into consideration the things that a firefighter does right and point them out. You will find that by doing so, it will help the individual relax and be more open to hear what you say next.

2. Criticize the act, not the person. There is a difference. If this is a first offense and you immediately criticize the person, you are going to form a hostile working environment. If you want to make your crew fear and dislike you, that's your prerogative, but as firefighters, we should never lose sight of the fact we may, one day, put our lives on the line for each other. That alone should be reason enough for you to want to foster a mutually respectful relationship.

3. Clearly explain what you want (and expect). Clarity is everything. Explain to the individual why his or her actions were wrong, and describe how you would like to see things done differently from here on out. If you have SOPs and organizational policies, use them as aids. Most people retain more of what they *read* than what they *hear*. Make sure the individual leaves the meeting with a clear understanding of what is expected.

4. Develop a solution together and agree on it. Firefighters are problem solvers. They like to play a part in solving their own problems. This helps them establish a sense of ownership. You probably don't like being dictated to, and neither do the people around you, but let's be honest, there are times you will need to do just that—after all, you are the company officer. If this is not one of those times, try working together. You'll find that most people will respond better to the latter method.

5. End on a positive note. You said what you needed to say; there's no need to belabor the point. End the meeting the way you began it, on a positive note. This will show the individual that you are willing to put the incident behind you and start fresh. Again, you will find that most firefighters will appreciate you more for doing so. The results should speak for themselves.

The steps outlined here work well, but if you find yourself dealing with an individual who simply will not change or correct what is considered an unacceptable practice, or if the person performed in a way that required stronger action than a simple critique, consult with your immediate supervisor regarding what actions you should take.

Fireproof Tip

The format outlined here is commonly referred to as the *sandwich technique*. This is when you place the performance issue in between two compliments. Doing so will help the individual relax, so he or she will be more open to hear what you say next.

Freelancing

Freelancing is one of the most dangerous, destructive, and counter-productive acts an individual—or group of individuals—can do in the fireground (fig. 3–9).

Fig. 3–9. Freelancing on the fireground can be disastrous and deadly and is not tolerated within the fire service.

The term *freelancing* is not the same in the fire service as it in the corporate world. In corporate America, freelancing is a term used for a person whose skills are available for hire, such as a freelance writer or photographer. On the fireground, however, freelancing occurs when a person works outside of an established action plan. When a person or group acts in ways that the incident commander is not aware of, they are freelancing. When acting in a way that contradicts a department's SOPs without being assigned to that task by a member of the command staff, a person has stepped away from the game plan and begun freelancing.

Simply put, if the IC cannot account for or track an individual or a company, those people are freelancing.

To illustrate why freelancing is a problem, consider the following scenario.

> Dave is a three-year veteran on his department. His four-member engine company arrived on the scene of a warehouse fire and reported to the IC for their assignment. They were the second engine company to arrive on the scene. They were given the task of securing a secondary water supply from a nearby hydrant, and stretching a $2\frac{1}{2}$-inch hose line into the structure as a backup for the first line, which was already in operation. Warehouse fires require a lot of water, and the line they were stretching is heavy and difficult to maneuver with just two people. The driver, as always, stayed with the engine to operate the pump and ensure the others received water. Dave's initial job was to connect the supply line to the hydrant so the engine could pump a continuous supply of water to the hose line. As he was doing this, the captain and another firefighter—the nozzle operator—began to stretch the line into the smoky structure, where visibility was less than 10%. After securing the supply line, Dave was told to follow the line into the structure and meet up with his captain so they could complete their task of backing up the first line and help extinguish the fire.
>
> Ten minutes had gone by and Dave had not reunited with his crew. This was far too much time and the captain knew it. Something must have gone wrong, otherwise Dave would have met up with them by now. The captain radioed Dave to ask where his location was. There was no response. The driver heard the transmission and radioed back that Dave had completed his first assignment (securing the water supply) then disappeared. He assumed Dave was somewhere inside the structure. The captain and the nozzle operator, who were now running low on air, left their line and exited the building to find Dave. Because the captain could not locate Dave, he transmitted an urgent radio message stating that a firefighter was unaccounted for. This halted all operations because the other firefighters on the fireground heard the transmission and began to look for the lost firefighter. Once outside of the structure, the captain found

Dave. He was working with a ladder company that was trying to force open some steel roll-down doors on a loading dock for ventilation purposes. He did not realize his radio was turned off.

Dave said he had forgotten to turn on his radio, and he was helping the ladder company because it looked like they could use another pair of hands. The other members of the ladder company were so focused on their job that they did not realize they picked up an extra man. Dave was safe, but his freelancing caused many problems at this fire: The initial engine company was placed in a dangerous situation because they were still inside the structure without a backup line. The incident commander has to change his overall tactics from fighting the fire to a firefighter rescue mission. Other firefighters on the scene stopped what they were doing when they heard the urgent message. As a result, the fire grew larger, and they ended up losing the warehouse. The entire mission was compromised and ultimately failed because of Dave's actions.

Freelancing is not tolerated in the fire service. It is a key ingredient, and sometimes the only ingredient, in a recipe for disaster. Incident commanders, officers, and firefighters all have the responsibility to ensure that team integrity is maintained at all times. Although there are different theories as to who should shoulder the blame when freelancing occurs (a renegade firefighter, a weak company officer, poor training), the chances of freelancing diminish greatly when all members on a team understand the mission they are trying to accomplish. In short, many times freelancing is a result of poor communication.

"Whether it's the fire service, organized sports, or the business world, when one team member freelances, the entire team mission is compromised."

In addition to the many problems that freelancing causes on the fireground, there is another negative by-product of freelancing that should be mentioned. If individuals consistently neglect their duties and tend not to be where they were supposed to be on a regular basis, the worst possible adjective in the world of firefighting is often used to describe them—coward. As terrible as this may sound, it's true. And once someone in the fire service is tagged with this title, he or she will spend the rest of a career trying to prove otherwise. In business, a person who neglects his or her duties may be called something else, perhaps incompetent. Right or wrong, that's just the way it is. As a leader, you could help your company members avoid this fate by taking actions to prevent freelancing from occurring in the first place.

How to prevent freelancing

To prevent freelancing from occurring in the future, you first have to determine how and why it occurred on your team in the first place. Begin by asking yourself the following questions:

- Is freelancing common on my team?
- When freelancing occurs, is it addressed?
- If so, how is it addressed?
- Who is held accountable?

If freelancing does not occur on your team, a smart leader should still take time to consider how he or she would address freelancing before, during, and after an incident.

It is easy to blame an individual for freelancing, but many times, that's taking the easy way out. I believe that an individual is rarely better than the organization he or she belongs to. In other words, if freelancing occurs on a regular basis, it's likely the organization's fault. It is the organization's responsibility from day one to establish the correct expectations. Poor performers can be a result of poor direction. As a company officer, there is one big caveat to this fact. Once you blame your organization, you are headed for supervisory disaster. To the others, *you* are the organization. The blame game never works. Instead of wasting your time and energy pointing fingers, take ownership of your team by setting the right tone and expectations from the beginning. Why?

Because, as I've mentioned before, the world has too many problem finders, we need more problem solvers. Also consider the fact that people who point their finger at others often fail to realize that three fingers on that same hand are pointing back at them.

....

"The world has too many problem finders.

We need more problem solvers."

....

To get to the root of the problem, use the 3U method. Determine whether freelancers are unaware of what they're doing, unwilling to change their ways, or unable to correct the problem.

The act of freelancing can be prevented by taking the following actions:

- **Train.** Prepare your team for success by ensuring that each person knows what to do when presented with common scenarios. This begins with reviewing your organization's policies and procedures (or standard operating procedures—SOPs) and other related documents. Then, practice daily. Training will take the guesswork out of the equation so that there are no misunderstandings when it matters the most.

- **Follow up in writing.** Training is fantastic, but follow-up is just as important. Work with your organization to help communicate the mission you are trying to accomplish. Once procedures are created or revised and/or training notices are sent out on paper, people are more likely to understand and follow through with their given assignments.

- **Give clear directions.** When you assign a task to someone, ask him or her to repeat it back to you so you can be assured that the assignment and your expectations are clearly understood. Clarity is everything.

- **Openly delegate tasks.** Each member of a team will have an assigned function, and all team members should know their own assignment as well as everyone else's. This will prevent two members from unknowingly working on the same task and duplicating their efforts ineffectively.

- **Track your personnel.** On the fireground, we use an accountability board to track what assignments were given out and to whom, where people are working, what resources are on scene and/or available, and any valuable information that may affect the outcome of the operation (figs. 3–10 and 3–11). The same type of system can be adapted to tackle administrative tasks.

- **Hold people accountable for actions.** When someone does go off and freelance, address it properly and professionally. Failure to do so is equivalent to giving your entire team permission to do whatever they want, whenever they want.

- **Communicate your expectations regularly.** Don't assume everyone knows what to do at all times. The job of a leader is to provide direction and help keep people focused on their tasks. You will know when someone has fallen off track. If you are unsure, follow your gut. If it looks and feels wrong, it probably is. Fix it—that's what a strong leader does.

Fireproof Tip

Although there are different theories as to who should shoulder the blame when freelancing occurs, many times the act of freelancing is a result of poor communication. When you assign a task to someone, ask him or her to repeat it back to you so you can be assured that the assignment and your expectations are clearly understood. Clarity is everything.

In the fire service, we understand that freelancing can be addressed and fixed in a soft environment (around the firehouse) easier that it can in a hard environment (on the fireground). We also understand that in our profession, freelancing can be deadly. Ask any organization that experienced a firefighter casualty because of freelancing if it wishes it could go back and address the issue long before the incident occurred and you will understand how important early training and prevention is. Freelancing may not result in a casualty within your organization, but it sure could contribute to overall team failure.

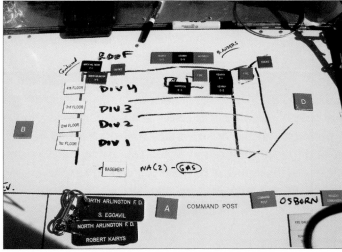

Figs. 3–10 and 3–11. Accountability boards can be used to track what assignments were given out, where people are working, what resources are on scene, and other valuable information that may affect the outcome at a fire. The same type of system can be used to track administrative tasks.

Mentoring

All great fire departments have some form of a mentorship program. It's arguably the best way to train new officers and/or compensate for the inevitable loss of experience, skill, and knowledge that occurs when senior members retire and probationary firefighters take their places. In a perfect world, veterans will have ample time to work with *probies* and pass on valuable information, but this isn't always the case. As I was writing this book, fire departments across the country were in the midst of facing abnormally high turnover rates, resulting in the loss of seasoned firefighters whose financially challenged municipalities weren't as quick to replace as they had been in previous years. This practice affects the transfer of knowledge as well as the preservation of fire service traditions and values.

If your organization doesn't have a formal mentorship program, the first step is to identify the challenges your department, as a whole, is facing. Perhaps morale is down. Maybe the overall performance of a specific group is unacceptable. Or maybe everything is running perfectly and you want to train your new recruit(s) to the high standard that others have previously set. Whatever your reason or challenge, the goal should be to prepare your team for victory and encourage new recruits and new leaders to step up. This, in part, is what a mentorship program can help you do.

A mentorship program can be specifically designed for many purposes, including the following:

- Educate and prepare new hires for the job by developing their skill set.

- Instill the right values and improve the attitude and performance of the mentees.

- Help preserve the rich history and traditions that your organization is known for.

- Provide a program, standard, and mechanism for evaluation of specific members.

- Encourage all members to be proactive in developing the overall team.

- Increase confidence levels of all who participate in the program.

- Increase morale by getting others involved.

Some fire departments have designed mentorship programs around new firefighters; others focus on preparing new officers to make the transition from firefighter to company leader and help develop their field-leadership and critical decision-making skills. A truly great department will have both. If your organization isn't sold on the idea of this type of program, that doesn't mean you can't develop one specific for the team of individuals that you are leading.

A critical step in developing a mentorship program is to first admit that you alone do not determine your department's or company's success. Your success will ultimately be determined by the collective efforts of your overall team; therefore, your effectiveness will multiply if you develop and implement a quality program.

At a young age you learned about inertia: objects in motion tend to stay in motion and objects at rest will remain at rest until an outside force moves them. This is as true with people as it is with a ball rolling down a steep hill. Mentors should understand that their job is to be that outside force that moves another person (or other people) to take appropriate actions.

As a leader, you may choose to personally mentor a specific individual, but this isn't always the best option. For example, in the fire service, there are too many responsibilities an officer will have that go beyond teaching a probie how to pack hose or do housework. Although a mentorship program will do far more than that, it's a wise move to use the resources you have available. With this thought in mind, I believe the best method is to match experienced firefighters with new recruits (fig. 3–12). This will provide you with a great opportunity to get more members involved.

Qualities of a good mentor

Mentors should possess certain qualities. They must be experienced in what they are teaching, goal oriented, calm, caring, positive, and honest. A mentor must also demonstrate strong communication abilities and be available for interaction on a daily basis. Not being available

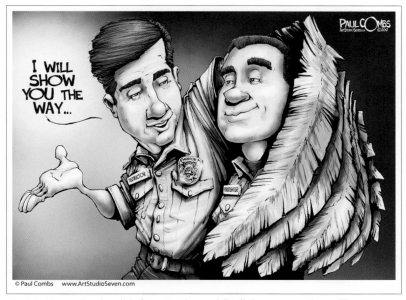

Fig. 3–12. Mentoring is a job for experienced firefighters as well as officers.

to provide counsel and guidance will ultimately end up defeating the purpose of a mentorship program. Additional qualities a good mentor should possess are:

- Adequate to above-average training, coaching, and counseling skills
- A history of a strong work ethic and positive attitude
- A belief in the mentorship program and a commitment to organizational development
- The ability to relate with and respect others, regardless of personal differences or rank
- A good understanding of the goals of your company and organization

The goal is simple: find the right mentor who can instill the right attitude, teach the right things, and prepare his or her mentee to do the job correctly. This is best accomplished by matching the mentee with someone who has been doing that job correctly for years.

....

"Mentors can make a powerful difference within your organization. It's easy to cut an apple and see how many seeds are in it, but there's no way of telling how many apples can come from just one seed."

....

How many individuals can one person mentor? This is a difficult question to answer without knowing the particulars of your organization, but many experts in the fire service and in corporate America believe the ideal number is somewhere between one and five. Five "key individuals" seems to be the maximum that a good mentor can handle before being spread too thin. The problem is, key people don't have the words "I'm a key person" tattooed on their forehead. You have to first identify them.

What to look for in a mentee/protégé

It goes without saying that most of the time we in the fire service may not have a choice. The probationary firefighter will be the one we want to work on developing. This is obvious. But let's say your organization is encountering the challenge of overall poor work performance. In that circumstance, you may want to choose specific individuals to train. If this is the case, consider the following. Your overall objective is to reduce the learning curve, motivate, and equip others with the tools they will need in order to reach their full potential. Doing so will not only benefit them, but the team as a whole. With this in mind, here are eight things to look for when choosing a mentee.

1. **Eager to grow/change.** Desire is the key to motivation, and motivation is the key to change. The person you choose absolutely must be willing to grow and should have accepted

the fact that "for things to change, *I* have to change." Being eager to grow and change also means the person is teachable, which only occurs when the he or she is humble enough to admit to not having all the answers.

2. **Willing to invest time.** We're all busy, but busy people are the ones who get things done. Look for busy people, but not people who are too busy doing destructive activities that aren't consistent with those of a successful person. If the person is disrespectful and acts as if he or she doesn't have time to meet with or talk with you, this is a problem that goes beyond mentoring and should be dealt with accordingly. You should seek to mentor people who would value this time and *act* on the knowledge that is passed down to them.

3. **A positive attitude.** Without the right attitude, the efforts of a mentor will be wasted. The mentee should be excited about the opportunity that he or she is being given. It makes sense to choose a person who is coachable and wise enough to recognize that there is no future in any job. The future of your organization is in the attitude of the person who holds the job.

4. **Respectful.** Few things are more bothersome than putting forth an effort that is unmatched by the person you are trying to help. A respectful person is one who appreciates the fact that others (in this case, you) see promise in them.

5. **Purposeful.** Does the prospective mentee have a specific intent to apply what he or she receives from you? If not, you run the risk of spending your quality time with the wrong person. To have purpose means the mentee is willing to work in a way consistent with achieving the desired end result.

6. **Confident.** This is the least important of the eight because many times, confidence comes with knowledge, and that's what the mentor will be providing. With that said, every successful person must have some semblance of confidence. Success and confidence go hand in hand. People are just naturally attracted to someone who is confident and in control.

7. **Loyal.** Investing time and effort on someone who has not displayed a sense of loyalty to your organization could come

back to bite you in the end. Loyalty should not only be a requirement for those who join your department, it is also a requirement for success in general. Master motivator Zig Ziglar went as far as to say, "Loyalty is the number one key to success."

8. **Willing to be accountable.** Accountability is the best way to measure the progress of a mentor's work. Accountability is the modern-day form of a progress report. Mentors and their protégés should communicate regularly to ensure the actions the mentee is taking are those that will produce the results that benefit the mentor, the mentee, your company, and the department as a whole.

When choosing the individuals to be mentored in your program, remember that these people are your ladder to success. Investing in them will provide a win-win scenario, benefiting you and your organization as much as it does them (fig. 3–13).

Fig. 3–13. Investing in the right people will benefit you, the individual, and the organization as a whole.

How to mentor

With respect to mentoring, the first rule cannot be overlooked: *begin with the end in mind*. In other words, you must have a clear picture of what you want your protégés to become. To do this, you must clearly communicate those intentions to the mentee, who should have the same end goal. Once this is established, you can begin the process of mentoring. The following are some suggestions to help get a mentor started. Here are six steps to effectively begin mentoring:

1. **Choose your mentees.** Using the selection process outlined above, choose the individuals who would benefit the most from this program. Again, you may not have a choice (probationary firefighters are the obvious individuals who need this type of program). Either way, you should still follow these steps.

2. **Begin the connecting process.** Reach out to the mentees and discuss your intentions. Make sure this individual, or group of individuals, are on the same page as you. Clarity is the key. The goal is to connect, communicate, then train regularly.

3. **Begin to equip them.** Once you know what talents, skills, and abilities your mentee(s) possess, and you have discussed the end result you are both seeking, it's time to equip them with whatever tools they are missing. Leading by example is often the best way to equip someone with the desire to improve. I would again encourage you to use the simple four-step process I provided previously when teaching mentees how to do a specific task. That process is:

   a. You do it, they watch.
   b. You do it along with them.
   c. They do it, you watch.
   d. You let them do the task alone.

4. **Enable them!** Let mentees see what they can become. Elevate and empower them to do more by giving them more responsibility. Give them the opportunity to fail, and teach them the right attitude about failure. Explain that the greatest successes in history often result from the biggest failures. These people ultimately succeeded because they never gave up.

5. **Encourage them!** Mentoring is a source of positive reinforcement. Encouragement will breed courage. I have often said and wholeheartedly agree that people will rise or fall to meet your level of expectations for them. Also remember that you should always affirm publicly.

6. **Inspire and encourage them to be self-motivated.** You can do this by casting a vision. Intimidation doesn't motivate people, but accomplishing their dreams and goals does. Once you discover what a person wants, use that to provide fuel for the fire—and to inspire! If you are an officer mentoring a firefighter who wants to also become an officer, that alone could be the motivation the individual needs to stay focused.

"People will rise or fall to meet your level of expectations for them."

People rarely improve when they only have themselves to copy. When it comes to mentoring, remember that those who surround themselves with people who are smarter, more talented, and just as driven profoundly increase their chances of success. Don't ever reach a point in your career where you foolishly believe you don't need a mentor of your own. Every day, remind yourself that you will not learn anything new by talking. If you are going to learn anything at all, it will be through asking the right questions to the right people, and listening.

Counseling

Counseling, although similar to mentoring, is different in important ways. In the fire service, counseling is offered when personal issues affect an individual's work performance. Recognizing when counseling is needed and proactively addressing the issue without being intrusive requires greater knowledge and skills than an average team leader possesses. As a mentor, or company officer, when you become aware that the performance of one of your department members is being affected by personal issues, it is wise to take that person aside and ask if there is anything he or she needs to talk about. Based on the answer you receive, you should be able to determine if this is an issue you can help by following the steps above or if this is a case in which professional counseling is needed. If it's the latter, it's best to offer support, follow your departmental policies, and leave professional counseling to the professionals.

Fireproof Tip

A critical step in developing a mentorship program is first to admit that your organization's success is not determined by you alone, but will ultimately be determined by the collective efforts of your overall team. Your effectiveness will multiply if you develop a program that develops others.

Improving Morale

One day my brother Joe and I were discussing morale. Joe is also a deputy chief in the fire service with a lot of experience and an incredible passion for the job. The eight suggestions in this section were a result of that conversation.

We are fortunate in our profession that the majority of firefighters are happy to be on the job and thoroughly enjoy coming to work; however, there is a minority who are dissatisfied and disgruntled. Unfortunately, in most cases the disgruntled always seem to be the most vocal. Over time, those voices seem to multiply (after all, misery loves company), and morale begins decreasing to obviously low levels. Take for example, a 100-member organization. If, out of 100, you have 10 chronic complainers, 30 happy (but less vocal) individuals, and 60 who are caught in the middle, the 10 complainers typically have the edge on converting the middle 60. This is as much a problem in any organization as it is in the fire service, but there is a solution. A strong leader, regardless of rank or position, can take charge of the situation and begin to take actions that will ultimately raise your organizations overall morale level.

Why is high morale important?

When firefighters are happy and morale is high, customers receive better service; accidents and injuries decrease; and grievances, discipline issues, and absenteeism are minimized (fig. 3–14). When morale is low, you'll see signs of reduced work ethic, increased violence, increased absenteeism, and sabotage. Some may even express a desire to quit altogether, which ultimately leads to a decrease in customer service and an increase in complaints. Poor morale will make employees turn on one another and play the blame game. Firefighters blame captains, captains blame chiefs, and chiefs blame firefighters. While many want to improve organizational morale, there are those who simply say, "It is what it is." Although it may be difficult for a probationary firefighter to increase the morale of others, every firefighter is responsible for his or her actions, and every individual's actions are part of the overall level of morale around the workplace. It's been said that the number one cause of low morale in the workplace is when people have to "drag around" dead weight, otherwise known as lazy coworkers no one will discipline. To solve this problem, a leader must step up and begin to develop an atmosphere where all members enjoy coming to work.

Fig. 3–14. When workers are happy, morale is improved and customers receive better service.

So, where do you begin? Below are eight proven steps that a leader can take to increase morale.

1. **Praise often and in public.** It's okay to catch someone doing the right thing, and when you do, it's also okay to let them know. Your words make a difference. Other than financial security, one of the biggest reasons an individual takes on a job is for recognition. Hearing the words "you did a great job" or "that was a nice stop" can mean more to a person than you think, especially when those words are spoken in the presence of others. When a firefighter performs well, I tell him or her so that everyone knows what was done correctly and that they too can strive to accomplish similar tasks. In the book *How to Win Friends and Influence People*, Dale Carnegie says to praise even the slightest improvements, and do it openly. When criticism is in order, it should be done in private. Don't be fooled by the term *constructive criticism*, because even those who sincerely ask for constructive criticism are secretly looking and hoping for praise. As a leader, it takes energy and commitment to deliver consistent uplifting service, but don't ever forget that when it comes to organizational success (especially in the fire service) praise is the spark that lights the fire.

2. **Set goals.** Business leaders, sports leaders, and the National Fire Academy would all agree that a true leader adopts a vision. A vision, which can be defined in a mission statement, cannot be met without clear and precise goals. Establish and define clear goals you want to reach as a unit, team, and/or department. Once the goals have been defined, take actions that are consistent with accomplishing them and encourage others within your organization to do the same. Establish expectations up front and measure performances accordingly. Be sure to praise members as goals and objectives are being met. Think of it this way: Not having a goal is like jumping in the car with your family for a road trip and not knowing which direction you want to travel. If you don't know where you're going, how could you expect to get there?

3. **Lead by example.** Demand the most from yourself as a leader. Provide the best training you can for your team. The better trained everyone is, the more confident and less worried they will be. As with goal setting, get others involved so they can be part of organizing important training and planning events. Showing that you have confidence in your team is a morale builder for them. A leader should also establish and maintain consistency in areas such as vision, reward, discipline, and attitude. It's essential that a leader be consistent with his or her mood. Don't be a Dr. Jekyll/Mr. Hyde. If you have personal challenges happening at home, seek professional help and solutions if you must, but don't let problems enter the workplace that negatively affect your mood or the mood of others you work with.

4. **Don't be a micromanager.** Ken Blanchard, in his book *The One Minute Manager*, tells the story of a boss who effectively manages a large team. One of his secrets is to get together with his key players each morning for one-minute meetings. During those meetings he communicates what he wants to accomplish for the day and leaves it up to those individuals to get the job done. He doesn't constantly look over their shoulders, keep them in unnecessary hour-long meetings, or criticize the way they accomplished the goal. He simply gives them direction and sets the ball in motion. The moral of the story is, do not micromanage. Respect the talents and abilities of others around you, and they will rise to meet your expectations of them. It's okay to give directions, but remember that it's the end result you are looking for. There is more than one way to tie a knot, and there is also more than one way to accomplish a task. Let others do their jobs and report to you at the end of the day or in the time frame you wanted that task accomplished. Some firefighters in leadership roles don't even realize that they treat their subordinates as liabilities rather than assets. Let people do their jobs and learn and make mistakes on their own. If you constantly criticize and micromanage, they will begin to lose confidence in themselves and respect in you.

5. **Eliminate problems quickly.** The majority of morale-killing problems we have in the fire service revolve around gossip

and rumors. If negative and often inaccurate rumors build, they can have far-reaching and negative effects on others— especially if that rumor revolves around transfers, layoffs, wage freezes, demotions, or disciplinary actions. When my brother and I were probationary firefighters, we spent our entire first year thinking that the governing body of our town was going to lay us off at any given moment. We later found out that this was not the case, and we learned an important lesson on the evolution of gossip. There have been three waves of spreading gossip over the last 100 years: "telegraph, telephone, and tell-a-fireman." Gossip and rumors can kill morale and fuel resentment faster than anything else, and the sad part is we do it to ourselves. The solution is simple: tell the truth and stop the rumor mill. Don't let group or individual concerns linger. Have an open-door policy and listen to the concerns of your coworkers. Serious problems, of course, would require chain of command, correct disciplinary action steps, and due process if necessary. However, most of what we encounter is not serious at all, unless, of course, we ignore it and let it grow to become serious.

6. **Encourage promotion and help your members advance in career** (fig. 3–15). I bet you didn't see this one coming. This doesn't mean you should provide certain individuals with special treatment or share promotional secrets while at work. This also doesn't mean that you should help others advance in rank at the expense of your own advancement. This means that you sincerely care about those you work with and create a working environment that provides them with time to develop new skills, study, and work toward promotion. As deputy chiefs, my brother and I both have captains on our tours who we would hate to lose, but they would make great chief officers and we would love to see them move up to that rank. When a position is open and an individual who works under you becomes the front runner for that position, be sure to help him or her learn the job duties of that title so that when promotion does happen, he or she can make a seamless transition. Leaders don't create followers; leaders create more leaders. Be enthusiastic about the success of others. Recognize

the potential in others and help them achieve it. Treat people as if they were what they should be, and by doing so you'll help them become what they are capable of becoming. If you do this, you will always have their loyalty and respect.

....

"Leaders don't create followers;

leaders create more leaders."

....

Fig. 3–15. Be enthusiastic about the success of others. Leaders don't create followers; leaders create more leaders.

7. **Instill team spirit.** There are a few ways to create a *team* attitude. As firefighters, we can train together and often create friendly competition between members. We can also include others in the process of making decisions that affect the organization as a whole. The key is to encourage all members to get involved. When training and developing solutions for problems, take advantage of the strengths and talents of those around you. If a firefighter has a background in building construction or teaches classes at a local fire academy, it benefits everyone to let that person share his or her expertise with other members. On that note, I encourage leaders within the fire industry to stress the point that a firefighter of any rank should not hold back information that can help educate coworkers, and an officer should not feel threatened when others do so. Sharing information should be encouraged. Great leaders know that to lead people, you have to sometimes walk behind them and give them their moment to shine. It's amazing what you can accomplish when you let others get the credit. Another great way to instill team spirit is to allow teams to create their own identity. This could come in the form of a logo or motto. Once chosen and approved, a tasteful logo could be put on T-shirts, hats, or as often seen in fire departments, on the apparatus they ride on. This, of course, should only be done with the permission of your department head.

8. **Be consistent and fair**. This holds true with respect to both rewards and discipline. Morale runs low when upper management shows favoritism. It's blatantly obvious when a leader treats people differently and gives one or two special treatment. You may have graduated from high school with one of your coworkers, and he may even be your best friend outside the job, but if his actions call for either reward or discipline, he should receive the same treatment as any other member. Being consistent and fair will assure that no member feels expendable or less valuable than another. Once favoritism is shown, it's a difficult task to regain the trust of the rest of the team. We must maintain a professional and respectful relationship with open and equal lines of communication for all members, and as leader, those around you need to know they

will all be treated fairly in accordance with your organization's rules and regulations.

We may all be macho "brave firefighters," but we're really just people who share a basic need of wanting to feel respected. When an individual feels like a key player who adds value to a team, that person will begin to perform at his or her best, which will increase the performance and working environment for all.

Fireproof Tip

Begin implementing these eight steps today and you will see an improvement in the morale of your organization. Once morale is increased, monitor it and don't ever stop pursuing 100% satisfaction among personnel. It may not be possible, but it's a goal worth pursuing.

Praise and Recognition

The three top reasons a person works are money, security, and self-esteem. People may initially take on a job for the monetary benefits it may provide, but without respect they will grow disenchanted. Praise and recognition are rewards that provide an awesome return on investment because they fulfill basic human needs—to feel accepted, valuable, and appreciated.

I do not want to sugarcoat an important point, so here's the reality. As a leader, if you don't provide some form of recognition for your hard-working team members, they will eventually want to leave and go work for someone who does. This is as true in the fire service as it is in the corporate world. I know firefighters who have transferred to other departments knowing they were going to make less money because they felt they were going to be treated with more respect.

Praising and recognizing people for a job well done is most effective when the act is performed in front of others. This can be done in formal and/or informal settings. Formal recognition occurs in ceremonies, events, and staff meetings (fig. 3–16). Informal recognition is usually immediate, on the spot, and in public. When individuals and teams do something really worthwhile, a strong leader will make a big deal out of it. Celebrate the successes and achievements of your colleagues. Put a lot of effort into recognizing others. Recognition is vital, but to be effective it must be positive, sincere, and timely.

Fig. 3–16. FDNY member receiving an award from Mayor Michael Bloomberg

I read an article in *USA Today* several years ago that stated the two most underused words in corporate America are "thank you." That's a shame, and it's a result of poor leadership. If you want to develop a productive team with positive energy, set goals, encourage those who are working hard and making good decisions, and publicly recognize people who do things exceptionally well and achieve high levels of success. People will not only feel appreciated, they're likely to go out and do it again.

Rewarding the members of your team for both their visible and less obvious contributions and achievements is an important way to foster greater mutual confidence. I have always encouraged my officers to show appreciation to the firefighters they supervise as often as possible. When they show appreciation, they get it in return, resulting in a positive working environment for everyone.

Years ago, I helped develop a meritorious act and commendations program for my organization. The program was created to reward members for exceptional acts performed while on or off duty. It is an internal program where nominations come from peers and are voted on by a meritorious acts review board (MARB), a committee that consisted of a handful of firefighters of various ranks.

Firefighters could be nominated for a variety of acts that involved risks that were considered beyond the ordinary, since the firefighter's task is inherently fraught with danger. The highest honor would involve an extremely high risk and result in the saving of a life. We also offered unit citations, academy standout, volunteer service, and firefighter of the year awards.

When it is found that the actions of the member(s) being evaluated did in fact prove to be worthy of an award, a citation bar, along with a letter from the MARB or the chief of the department (describing the reasons for the award), would be presented to the deserving individual or group. A copy of that letter is also forwarded to the mayor and town council members. The citation bar is provided so firefighters can display the award on their Class A dress uniforms.

This program provides our organization a way to show appreciation for those who truly went above and beyond the call of duty. It lets the firefighters know that we appreciated them. I once heard it said that recognition is a powerful thing; babies cry for it and grown men die for it. Certainly, we do not want anyone ever to have to die for recognition, but wouldn't it be a shame if a person died without ever having received any?

There is only one caveat to praise and recognition. If you provide it unequally or undeservingly, it can have an adverse effect. Recognition is essential, but it must be warranted. With that said, get excited about giving credit to those who deserve it. Be on the lookout for all types of achievement, and when you witness or hear about it, acknowledge it (fig. 3–17).

Fig. 3–17. Acknowledge the actions and achievements of those who perform above and beyond the call of duty.

Two ways to show appreciation:

- Acknowledge deserving accomplishments early. Showing appreciation for a job well done can be a simple act like saying "thank you" or "great job" in an informal setting.

- Establish a time, place, and more formal method for acknowledging those who perform at a high level.

Keep a journal of accomplishments. Predetermine the level of appreciation you will consider for each level of accomplishment. Write down the names of everyone you want to acknowledge and list how their achievements enhance the performance of your team. In a formal setting, which could even be a meeting or a company party, provide the appropriate level of recognition for those who deserve it.

Be generous and sincere when you praise, and ensure others will take notice and duplicate the praiseworthy actions. Also, make sure you praise the act, not just the person.

Fireproof Tip

A significant task as a team leader is to find ways to show your appreciation for your team and motivate them to be the best they can be. Once you do, you will be amazed by what you can accomplish when you let others have the credit.

Performance Evaluations

A performance evaluation (PE) can be a great asset to help a leader express appreciation for an individual's efforts and contributions to the team.

Initiating PEs within your organization is a risky tactic if they are not implemented or conducted properly. Without explaining the goal of the PE, team members may think that these documents are there strictly as an accountability tool. Although accountability is one of the benefits of a PE—and a very necessary one within the fire service—that is only one reason these documents are effective. When used correctly, PEs can be a great tool for enhancing the working climate and providing recognition.

There are two main ways in which performance evaluations can benefit your team:

- They give you an opportunity to express appreciation. You already know the importance of recognition. PEs can be a way of measuring a person's improvement and provide encouragement for him or her to continue on a positive path. A by-product of recognition is a higher quality work environment. Who doesn't like being in the company of others who appreciate them?

- They help ensure accountability. As important as it is to praise someone for a job well done, it's equally important to address when a person consistently shows poor judgment or when policies are not being followed. Being soft on policy within the fire service is intolerable. PEs provide you with a better way to control and address the actions of your team members. This will enable you to enforce SOPs and ensure compliance. Many times you will find that people don't follow procedures because they were not aware of them. PEs are a way to identify these oversights and address them on a case-by-case basis. They give you more control over what's happening on your team and help you create more competent team players. In short, you can't fix it if you didn't know it's broken.

Performance evaluations can be a valuable tool, but you may encounter resentment if you place more emphasis on the accountability portion of the evaluation then you do in the recognition portion. Use PEs for both.

Fireproof Tip

Performance evaluations give you an opportunity to express appreciation when people do things correctly. They also enable you to hold people accountable when they do not and provide you with a tool to help you restore discipline by ensuring that the policies, procedures, and mission of your organization are being followed. A lack of discipline can be contagious, caustic, and destructive.

Conducting Effective Meetings

The word "effective" is the key when it comes to conducting meetings. Most organizations in America hold more meetings than necessary. Those meetings are also much longer than they need to be and not well organized or prepared. As important as meetings are to your organization, if done incorrectly, they will prove to be nothing more than a practical alternative to work. Gathering a group of people and having a meeting without an agenda is like staffing a fire engine after a call comes in and pulling out of the firehouse without any clue as to what your destination is going to be.

Great companies recognize the value of getting input from every member on their team, from the newest recruits and talent to the most senior members (fig. 3–18). Take a moment to consider the fact that the newest members on your department may have the most fresh and unique ideas. Sometimes those of us who have been around for a while are creatures of habit. Brainstorming solutions by gathering the input of all those affected by your decision will give you an edge and help everyone involved to buy into the process of whatever it is you are trying to accomplish. When your entire team is sold on an idea that they helped conceive, it has a substantially better chance of working.

Fig. 3–18. Great organizations understand that meetings provide the opportunity to get input from every member on the team.

Use a meeting agenda. This will enable you to keep the meeting on schedule, allow the team to prioritize items of concern, and provide for structure so that no members monopolize your time by getting off track with their thoughts and comments. Also, keep your meetings short, and stay focused on the reason why you are there. Nothing is worse than attending a staff meeting that goes an hour longer than it needed to and confuses everyone who was in attendance because there was no structure or development of a game plan. When scheduling a meeting, invite only those who are necessary. If you are addressing issues that concern only a portion of your department, such as officers and managers, the attendance of others who are not in those positions may hinder your ability to accomplish your overall goal and result in the meeting getting off track. Furthermore, those members could be out accomplishing other tasks and producing while the meeting is in session.

Here are a few surefire strategies to shortening your meetings to help ensure they are more effective.

1. **Start on time.** When it comes to meetings, live by the statement, "Don't punish the punctual." The day you begin to start meetings 5, 10, or 15 minutes late is the day you say to your team, "It's okay if you're late, we'll wait for you." The by-product of late meetings is a lackadaisical attitude that will carry over into other areas of performance. When a colleague of mine took over as the shift commander of his new tour, he shared a great story with me. He told his team that he would be having monthly meetings where they could get together and discuss important and relevant issues. The first meeting he scheduled came with a surprise; one of his officers was 15 minutes late. Instead of waiting, he locked his office door and started the meeting with the ones who were on time. When that officer knocked, he told him the meeting was already in progress and he'd have to wait until next month's meeting to join them. Neither the officer nor anyone else was ever late again. Although he admitted to me that this was uncomfortable for him to do, he certainly made his point.

2. **Don't sit down.** I remember talking with a friend who was thrilled to finally get a meeting with one of the wealthiest men in Boston. He wanted to pitch his services, so he worked day and night for three weeks to craft the "perfect" presentation. As the assistant walked him into the meeting room, he was thrown off when he noticed that the large board room had a table but no chairs. The multimillionaire entered the room, introduced himself, shook my friend's hand, and said, "You have five minutes. Tell me what brings you here." My friend

later found out that this is how the man did business: quick and to the point. When I bring my tour together for a meeting, I'm fine with them getting comfortable, but I like to stay on my feet, because it's a constant reminder that I have only a short amount of time to get to the task at hand. The more comfortable I make myself, the more off track the meeting tends to go.

3. **Be prepared.** This one may be a bit obvious, but sometimes common sense is not common practice. If you are going to bring your team together for a meeting, take time out of your busy schedule to prepare. If you don't develop an agenda, the meeting will seem unorganized, and you will begin to lose credibility as a leader. On the other side of the coin, the other attendees need to do their homework in advance as well. If I'm going to pull a team of firefighters together for a meeting on how we can better tackle wildland-urban interface fires, I'll let them know what the area of concern is going to be before the meeting so they can come in with some ideas. If you want to talk about improving customer relations, let your team know in advance so they can come to the meeting prepared with possible suggestions and solutions.

4. **Be clear and specific.** When an engine company arrives on the fire scene, they walk up to the incident commander and ask, "What do you need, Chief?" The IC has about 10 seconds to tell that company officer what he wants accomplished. There's no time to waste or hesitate. It's a clear, specific directive, based on goals and objectives. A team meeting should not be this one-sided, but it does need to be based on specific goals and objectives, which should be clearly stated at the beginning of the meeting (fig. 3–19). You absolutely do want feedback and opinions from the others in the room, but you will achieve far more productive results when you establish a clear sense of direction and focus, not to mention a more energized team, because no time will be wasted talking about or pursuing work that isn't relevant.

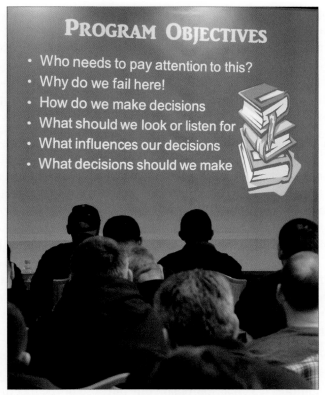

Fig. 3–19. The goals and objectives of a meeting should be clearly stated at the beginning.

5. **Stick to the agenda.** Only tackle topics you are prepared to handle. On the fireground, my department uses a command board that includes a dry-erase whiteboard where we can write down all relevant information. There is also a blank spot on the board that I use to jot down things that are relevant to our job as firefighters, but not relevant to the job were currently working at. I call it a parking lot. It can be used as a space to write things down so you can clear your mind of any possible distractions and address them later. For example, one afternoon we had a major explosion at an electricity-generating station in the industrial area of our town. The fire was significant and required a great deal of attention, but at that fire we

realized we were lacking pre-plans for this and many other facilities in that area. I wrote the word *pre-plan* on the board and forgot about it until I was cleaning up. At that point, I wrote "pre-plan" down on a note pad and began to organize thoughts for a meeting that took place at a later date where we discussed this issue. The same concept can be used in a team meeting. If a concerning issue arises and you don't have time to address it, document it in your parking lot and revisit it at a later date.

6. **Separate and subjugate.** This is just a fancy way to say divide and conquer. There will come times when some of the people in your meetings do not need to be there. If a person runs an engineering firm and she wants to discuss how she could improve sales, her technical people don't need to be in the room. The same could be said when a fire service leader is discussing engine and ladder company operations and fire prevention personnel are in the room. If you separate people into meetings that cover areas they need to be concerned with, you will be able to tackle the issues quickly and move on to your next task.

7. **Never end late.** Here it is in a nutshell. If you're having a 15-minute meeting, 10 minutes in, let the others know you have 5 minutes left to accomplish your purpose of the meeting. I have attended 30-minute meetings and wondered, after 90 minutes, why we hadn't even started to discuss the issues we were called in to discuss in the first place. This gave me the feeling that I was part of a disorganized team and working under an unfocused leader who didn't respect the time of others.

No one wants to spend more time than needed in unproductive meetings, and surely you'd rather have your team spend their time where it is most productive: training or accomplishing organizational goals. Shortening your meetings will play a big part in helping you stay focused and be a more effective leader.

Fireproof Tip

As important as meetings are to your organization, if done incorrectly, they will prove to be nothing more than a practical alternative to work. Use an agenda, eliminate distractions, and stay focused on the reason for the meeting.

Tackling Administrative Tasks and Creating Programs

I once wrote an article titled "The Simple Approach to Writing Standard Operating Procedures (SOPs)." In that article I outlined five steps that, when followed, will provide fire service leaders with a comprehensive format that can be used to develop and implement standard operating procedures, otherwise known as standard operating guidelines. Having written more than 50 guidelines for my department and coauthoring the book *Fireground Operational Guides*, I can say with confidence that those five simple steps can help anyone write a thorough and comprehensive SOP, regardless of whether he or she is a novice or a seasoned firefighter, even with limited writing experience.

The exciting thing about this format is it can be used for more than just developing SOPs; it can also be used as a guide when developing any type of program, whether it's a community awareness and education program, a public relations program, or a department-wide mandatory training class on any subject (fig. 3–20). With this thought in mind, I want to encourage you to consider the five-step outline in this section as an effective format that can be used not only within your organization for program development reasons, but also as a format for administrative tasks. These five steps can easily be remembered using the acronym P-R-DIE, which stands for Plan, Research, Develop, Implement, and Evaluate.

In the fire service, we are constantly developing and participating in programs that benefit our community. With that thought, let's say your organization is interested in initiating a public relations program that is designed to encourage young children to read. As a leader, you may be asked to develop a similar program one day. The following is an example of how you could approach this task using the proven P-R-DIE administrative format.

Fig. 3–20. The P-R-DIE format can be used when developing programs and/or organizing mandatory training such as the ladder rescue drill shown in this photo.

Step 1: Plan

You've already conducted a needs assessment, identified your problem, and come up with the solution of a public relations program. You should initiate this stage by forming a committee. It could have two members or more; the committee's size may vary. The members should be motivated and knowledgeable about the subject on which you are developing this program. For example, coworkers who have children or those with teaching experience should be considered. When choosing members for your committee, look outside of your organization for legal and expert opinions on the topic. Your committee should also include representatives of groups that will be affected by the program. In this example, local teachers or board of education members could provide valuable insights.

Once your committee is formed, schedule a meeting and choose a committee manager. This is the most effective way to facilitate coordination. As the individual responsible for developing the program, you should also assume the role of committee manager. At the meeting, effectively communicate the specific goals and objectives you are trying to meet so that all members have a clear understanding of the task at hand. Prescribe a course of action by delegating tasks; designate a time line for their completion. Early tasks are mainly fact-finding and research oriented, such as those outlined in Step 2. Members should write down their assignments so that there is no confusion about who is assigned which task. Document what occurred at the meeting, and prepare a report for your superior. These two actions should be taken after each of the five steps in the process.

Step 2: Research

It's imperative that the committee members research all facts that are pertinent to the development of this program. In this example, the best place to begin is by doing an Internet search of other successful reading programs such as "Read Across America." In short, seek help from those in the know.

It is also helpful to contact other local organizations to see if they have a program (or SOP) on the topic. You may also be able to do this with a simple Internet search, since many departments post their SOPs on their websites.

Call around and see who may already have developed and implemented a successful program. One simple call may provide you with 90% of the information needed. It's not always necessary to reinvent the wheel. In the fire service, we are not in competition with other departments. In other words, we are not in cutthroat corporate America where sharing information with a competitor is frowned upon and bad business. The brotherhood in the fire service is strong enough that firefighters willingly share information with other departments.

Research every aspect of the topic at hand, including the training of personnel or the purchasing of new equipment as well as all costs that will be involved. You will want to identify who your target audience is (for example, perhaps all the third graders that attend your local grammar schools). You also want to identify which individuals or combination of your workers and teachers will be interacting directly with the children. You also want to look into what types of books you want to read and whether you will be leaving additional books with the children after you leave.

Find out if there is money in the budget to cover the expenses or if there are grants or other means available to help your department offset those costs. Keep in mind that every member of the committee must realize that he or she is part of an overall team. Even if one person's area of research seems small in comparison to another, all members must be aware that each of them is responsible for providing a valuable piece to the puzzle.

Once the research is complete, the committee should meet again and move to Step 3.

Step 3: Develop

During this meeting, collect all the information that each committee member has acquired, put it on the table, and discuss it (fig. 3–21). At this point, the arranging of an overall program (perhaps in an SOP-type document) will usually fall on one person's shoulders, most likely yours. This is where the writing begins. Although that may seem intimidating, keep in mind that you are not writing a novel, you are simply developing an outline of procedures to follow.

The outline should clearly state the name of the program, the goals of the program, and the actions each person is expected to take in order to ensure success. Some of this has been done in the Research stage, but now is the time to fine-tune everything.

Indicate specific techniques and methods to follow in order for each individual involved to perform his or her tasks in a way that represents your organization properly and enables the program to accomplish its goals. There are various ways to format what you put down on paper. The most effective format is an SOP. An effective SOP includes the following sections: Purpose, Scope, Responsibility, and Procedures or Guidelines. At the very least, you want to make sure the document you develop includes:

- The reason the document was developed

- An outline of when and where this program and procedure shall apply

- A list of each person (or job title) who shares the responsibility of implementing the program

- Specific guidelines each participant must follow in order to ensure success

- A mechanism for evaluating the effectiveness of the program. (This will be discussed more in Steps 4 and 5.)

Once the document or SOP is formatted, have each committee member review it for accuracy, and ask other knowledgeable and willing team members or subject experts to proofread it. They can also check for inconsistencies. If you are like me, you spend so much time cutting and pasting sentences and paragraphs that you tend to make simple grammatical errors that are easily overlooked. A first-time reader is more likely to notice typos.

Fig. 3–21. Begin the development phase by reviewing and discussing the information that each committee member has collected.

Step 4: Implement

Implementing an important program should not be done without first evaluating its effectiveness. For example, choose one school to test your pilot program. Use this opportunity to work out any kinks. Utilize as many people as needed in order to assess whether you feel your efforts enabled you to meet your goals. Once this is complete, it's time to bring that document, and the pilot program results, to your superiors for review.

The committee or program manager should meet with the department head to review the final product and discuss the implementation process. This is usually done with a special notice with the new document attached. Include a date of implementation so there is no confusion about when the program initiation date becomes effective.

Once the program is established and implemented, everyone who is affected should review the written document. Remember that this is a public relations program. What good would it be if the public didn't know about it? With this in mind, the committee members should consider the best ways to spread the word. The following are some possible ways to inform the public of your new program:

- Local newspapers (contact the publisher or your community reporter)

- Local television programs (contact the program's producer)

- Brochures mailed to all local residents (there will be significant costs involved with this method)

- The Internet (post the program on your organization or community website; develop a page on popular social networks)

- Community notification channels on television and school handouts that teachers can give their students to bring home

You can choose one or all of these methods. Your best option would be a combination of those listed, otherwise known as a multimedia campaign. Whichever method you choose, be sure to include all essential information, such as program locations, times, and dates.

Step 5: Evaluate

A big mistake many organizations make comes a year or two after the implementation of a program. To prevent this, remember RER, which stands for review, evaluate, and revise. These three words are crucial in the fire service. We are constantly dealing with rapidly changing conditions on the fireground that make it essential that we review, evaluate, and revise our tactics regularly to ensure we are constantly meeting our goals of life safety, incident stabilization, and property conservation. As with fireground operations, when it comes to managing programs, the RER method will serve you well.

During the reviewing process, which may come one week or one year into the program, ask yourself or your committee simple questions such as: Is this program still an effective way to meet our objectives? Does this program contradict acceptable methods or public relations standards that are followed throughout the fire service? If you have developed an SOP, evaluate whether the SOP is still the "one best way" to accomplish the required task. The answers to these questions will determine if the program needs revision at that time. Also be sure to compare pre-program results with post-program results, and evaluate whether your department has been more effective since this procedure was implemented. In the scenario outlined in this article, the questions to ask are:

- Have you improved your relations with the public you serve?

- Have you accomplished your goals of encouraging young children to read?

After all, those were your two main goals. It is also imperative that your organization cycle any and all programs through the planning stage often to ensure they continue to meet their goals and objectives.

I'd like to share one more thought regarding the development of programs. A good leader will not forget to reward the committee members and others who helped to develop programs. Some organizations may go as far as to provide comp days or financial compensation (such as overtime) for those who spend time working on the program. This, however, is becoming less and less likely with the state of the economy. You may not have any control over how your organization rewards committee members, but you do have control over how *you* reward them. At the very least, a simple thank you can go a long way.

Communication and Presentations

I was in the training office when my chief came to me one morning and said, "I forgot to tell you yesterday. There is a meeting happening this morning that I need you to attend." He assured me that I would not have to say anything. He just wanted me to sit in and take notes. The meeting had already started, so I jumped in my car and hurried over.

When I arrived, I entered a room full of about 30 people, including the mayor and several council members, the police chief and representatives of several other local law enforcement agencies, the business administrator, the town engineer, and a bunch of lawyers. Before the door closed behind me, every eye in the room was on me and the mayor said, "Great, Chief Viscuso is here. He's representing our fire department. Let's get his point of view on this."

Have you ever seen the look of a deer in the headlights? My immediate response was, "Can you first bring me up to speed on what's been said so far?" The mayor talked about the discussion they were having about a freight train that was so long when it stopped in the train yard in South Kearny it would block several intersections, sometimes for as long as 15 minutes. I walked up to the map and begin to give a 10-minute presentation on the challenges our department faces as a result of this. After the meeting, I remembered two things. First, the mayor and attorneys for both the town and the business owner responsible for the train, thanking me and asking if they could call me to talk about solutions, and second, how grateful I was they didn't ask me what my thoughts were on the escalating violence in the North Kivu region of DR Congo.

My point is that a leader is often asked to speak and present in public—sometimes without a chance to prepare. Leaders must be good at communicating (fig. 3–22).

Fig. 3–22. Captain Bryan Emenecker is an example of someone with strong communication skills. Here he is speaking to a group of firefighters at a FireOpsOnline Seminar.

When it comes to speaking in public, having a vast knowledge base is essential, but without good communication skills, the thought of doing so can be daunting. Everyone knows the number one fear in America is public speaking; number two is death. I remember having breakfast with a friend one day when he jokingly said, "Don't you find it odd that most people would rather be the dead guy in the box than the guy giving the eulogy?" I'm pretty sure that was the first time coffee ever came out of my nose.

The cold, hard fact is that a person with an extensive knowledge base but poor communication skills is at the mercy of the lesser-educated person who knows how to communicate a message in a clear and confident manner. This also holds true for individuals who are taking promotional exams or interviews. Knowing the right answers is only half the battle; you also have to be able to communicate them the way a leader would. With that in mind, following are some pointers that will help you prepare for speaking in front of others.

Making the presentation

Imagine you are entering a room where you are expected give a 10- or 15-minute presentation (maybe to a group of coworkers, the public, or the upper management of your organization). Although the scenario may change, there are "absolutes" when it comes to making a good presentation, regardless of the setting and audience.

Good study habits and a strong work ethic will arm you with the knowledge base I mentioned earlier, but if you are serious about elevating yourself above the crowd and overcoming handicaps that most of us have, then you should be aware of the subconscious aspects of an oral presentation.

Subconscious aspects. When you are speaking, it's not only your words that people are paying attention to; it's also your voice, your body language, and your appearance. Here is a quick breakdown of all three:

- **Your voice.** *How* you say something is as important as *what* you are saying. It's essential to present yourself in a confident but not overconfident or arrogant manner.

- **Body language.** This is a subject in its own right and a topic about which much has been written and said. In essence, your body movements express what your attitudes and thoughts *really* are. On the following pages, I will share valuable tips on body language.

- **Appearance.** First impressions influence people's attitudes toward you. Dressing appropriately for an occasion is extremely important (for firefighters, this means a neatly pressed uniform). Being well groomed is also important. It's hard to take a person seriously when he looks like he just crawled out of bed.

As with most personal skills, oral communication skills cannot be handed to you. Others can only point the way. As always, *practice is essential* to improve your skills and equip you with the tools to provide the best presentation you are capable of.

Body language. Consider this. Words are not the only way people communicate when they are speaking. Beyond the *ums* and *ahs*, there are gestures and expressions that tell stories. With very few exceptions, people consistently communicate their inner feelings quite openly. Each gesture is like a word in a language, and regardless of whether you are aware of it, we all subconsciously speak that language.

Consider this for a moment. Everyone has a distinctive walk that makes him or her easily recognizable to their friends. In the book titled *How to Read a Person Like a Book*, authors Gerald I. Nierenberg and Henry H. Calero discuss *gesture clusters*, which enable people to read you. These clusters are a grouping of individual gestures that tell a story about you. If you're not careful, these clusters will cause your audience to judge you rather than listen to the words that are coming out of your mouth.

Here are a few examples. Imagine a man who is sitting rigid, in an upright position with ankles locked. His eyebrows are raised and his hands are clenched together making one big fist, and he is rhythmically massaging one thumb against the other. Alone, these gestures are not very telling; together, however, they send the message that this man is *nervous*.

Now imagine a woman who is sitting across the table from you who is unable to make eye contact. Instead, she is looking at the floor, her shoulders slumped. The woman is trying to tell you something, but she is clearly struggling to come up with words. It's obvious this woman *lacks confidence*.

In a third example, without saying one word, it's clear that the person who turns his back on you while you are talking and slams the door as he walks out of the room is *angry*.

You must be aware of what your body is saying. You should also be aware of single gestures that send a strong message to others in order to comprehend the full meaning of the gesture cluster and determine the congruity of its components. Take, for example, a person with arms folded high on his chest. This gesture is synonymous with stubbornness (think of a baseball umpire who is being yelled at by a manager). Let's look at several other types of nonverbal communication that are easily recognizable and often encountered:

- Frown: displeasure or confusion

- Raised eyebrows: fear, envy, or disbelief

- Hand to cheek: nervous, critical, pondering, or listening intently

- Inability to make eye contact: hiding something

- Touching/rubbing nose: doubt

- Covering your mouth: hiding something

- Pinching the bridge of your nose, eyes closed: self-conflict

- Clearing your throat (more than once): typically means anxious or apprehensive. This, however, is more than just a subconscious gesture. Mucus forms in the throat when a person becomes anxious or apprehensive. The natural thing to do when this occurs is clear your throat. The key is to prepare well enough so that you are less nervous.

Gesture clusters, together, will tell you a lot about a person, but when it comes to single gestures, facial expressions tend to be the dominant body gesture. When giving a presentation while sitting at a table, consider the fact that most of your body will be hidden behind the table. If you are sitting upright, which you should be, your facial expressions will be the most obvious gestures.

Top salespeople are well aware of the fact that a person's facial gestures are telling a story. When dealing with a prospect whose eyes are turned down and whose face is turned away, the salesperson knows he is being shut out. The same salesperson will recognize that the sale is virtually made when the prospect's head is shifted to the same level as hers and he is sharing an enthusiastic smile. When you are giving a presentation, or taking a promotional exam, your facial gestures play a much greater role than you would imagine. Your answers may be spot on, but if your expression says something different, it may affect someone's opinion of whether you are ready to step up.

Quick reference speaking tips. Here are eight tips to help you deliver your message in a confident, professional manner.

- Speak clearly and be natural.

- Don't shout or whisper. Make sure everyone in the room can hear you.

- Don't rush your words or talk deliberately slowly. It's okay to pause at key points to emphasize the importance of a particular point you are making; however, be aware of your time constraints.

- Don't try to be a flashy speaker. It's okay to change your delivery (speed, pitch of voice, etc.), but don't overdo it. This may work for motivational speakers, but it rarely does when giving a presentation.

- Keep hand movements to a minimum. Again, it's okay to sparingly use your hands to emphasize points, but don't indulge in too much animated hand waving. This can be irritating and distracting.

- Make eye contact. You can look down at your notes, but look at the people you are speaking to as much as possible. If there is more than one, don't fix on one individual. Eye contact projects confidence.

- Avoid nervous body movements (as described previously).

- Don't ramble. Make your point then move on to the next point(s). If you are asked questions, your answers should be concise and to the point.

Presentation aids. Props and presentation aids can be valuable tools depending on the scenario. If you are speaking about new tools, you will obviously want to display the tools so everyone can see what you are talking about. If you are using a PowerPoint presentation, make sure you rehearse your presentation using the projector and a screen (fig. 3–23). Oftentimes, presentations that look great on the computer monitor don't look as good when projected onto a screen.

Fig. 3–23. When using PowerPoint, be sure to rehearse your presentation using the projector and a screen prior to the day of your lecture.

Advice from a friend. I feel compelled to give my friends in the fire service a bit of advice that can help them prepare for a promotional exam.

When taking a promotional exam, you will probably not be provided any presentation aids other than your notes, which should be used for reference only. You may also be allowed to have a pen and stopwatch on hand. If so, place all three (your notes, pen, and stop watch) in front of you in an organized manner. When you walk into the testing room, the assessor may hand you notes and ask if they are yours. Quickly scan through them and make a mental note of what pages you have (if more than one). Place your pen and stopwatch on either side. If you are permitted to use a stopwatch, it will be for you to keep time. When the assessor signals that your testing period has begun, start the timer. This is something you should do whenever you are giving a timed presentation. It will allow you to stay on track and not go beyond your allotted time. Occasionally glance down at your watch to keep track of time. This is the same procedure you want to follow when practicing for your presentation. You don't want to fumble around trying to find the start button at the beginning of your presentation. This will make you look unprepared, disorganized, and nervous, all of which will negatively affect your overall presentation.

The same advice can be followed for anyone who is preparing for a job interview. Unless your last name is Hilton or Trump, success (or reality shows) in any arena is not handed to a person on a silver platter. If you are serious about advancing your career and achieving higher ranks, the first thing you should do is to identify the reason or reasons *why*. In other words, what is the driving reason you want to be a lieutenant, captain, battalion chief, deputy chief, or whatever other position you desire? Your answer may be self-fulfillment, money, or simply because you know you would make a great officer. The important thing is that you have an answer—a reason. Without it, you will likely find a reason why preparing, or studying, is more of an inconvenience than a necessity.

Once you identify that reason and have dedicated the necessary time reading the appropriate books (which is essential) and attending educational seminars (which is highly recommended), you can focus on three key things:

1. Practice,

2. Practice, *and*

3. Practice.

You don't want to make the mistake that so many others do, which is showing up on exam day unprepared. If the first time you give an oral presentation is on the day of your test, you are not playing your hand well. Instead of "winging it," prepare as if your career depends on it. I will admit to taking a mock test every day for 30 to 45 days prior to my deputy chief exam. On the day of the test, I was fully prepared to review my scenarios, organize their notes, and give my presentation.

What exactly are you preparing for? In short, you are preparing to hit the main points that will provide you with the best possible score, and you are preparing to deliver your message in the most professional manner possible.

Rehearsing your presentation. The best way to rehearse for a presentation that you have to give (either for a promotional exam or to a large audience) is by video- or audiotaping yourself as you practice. Ask a study partner or family member for help. You may find it difficult to watch or listen to yourself at first. After all, we are all our own worst critics. This step, however, is crucial because it will enable you to make adjustments and fine-tune your presentation. Look for the subconscious body movements and facial expressions on the videotape. Listen for voice inflections and verbal flaws (such as *ums* and *ahs*) on both a video- and audiotape. Don't get upset if you aren't perfect—you won't be—just remember that you only improve with practice.

Here is a simple daily ritual that you can use to help you prepare in the days leading up to a presentation:

1. Study your topic. You can *never* have enough knowledge.

2. Practice your delivery. Ask a friend, co-worker, or family member to watch. Tape your presentation so you can assess yourself.

3. Make adjustments to improve your presentation.

4. Repeat steps 1, 2, and 3 daily from now until your presentation. The more comfortable you are on the day of your presentation, the better off you will be.

Communicating on the fireground

I have already touched on communication and presentation skills, but I haven't placed the proper emphasis on it as an essential leadership skill in the field. Think about this: the receiver of a message usually takes the blame when things go wrong. In reality, the problem is oftentimes a result of the sender's inability to communicate a message properly. One of the most dangerous things on a fireground is poor communication. When firefighters don't know their assignment, or when engine and ladder company personnel are both unaware of what the other is doing, freelancing is inevitable, and nothing good will come of it.

If you are in charge at a fire scene (or taking the lead of a major project), you need to do two things very well: give precise directions, and listen (fig. 3–24).

Fig. 3–24. An incident commander needs to do two things very well: give precise directions, and listen.

If an incident commander is constantly barking orders but doesn't give his full attention to radio transmission or feedback from other officers, he is likely to miss valuable information. I remember conducting a post-incident analysis after a three-alarm fire when one officer came up to me and thanked me for acknowledging his radio transmissions. He told me that his previous shift commander never did that. Imagine being in a smoke-charged room with zero visibility. You discover something that concerns you, such as fire in the walls, and report back to your IC without his ever acknowledging you. Talk about feeling abandoned.

On the fireground, everyone, including the IC, should spend 80% of his or her time listening and only 20% talking. This is the same ratio we should use in life. One of the key ways we gather information that can help us make smart decisions is thorough listening. Unfortunately, listening is one of the most underdeveloped skills in our society. In our industry, communication is an overworked word but an underworked act. In my experience, I found this to be true in most other industries as well.

The bottom line is that you can improve your effectiveness as a leader (and your quality of life) by improving your communication skills.

Fireproof Tip

Leaders must be good at communicating. When it comes to giving a presentation, knowledge is power . . . but *only* if the presenter is a strong communicator who knows how to deliver a message. This can only be acquired through practice. Don't pass up the opportunity to speak to small groups whenever possible. This is a great way to hone your skills.

Acquiring Tools for Training

Every organization exists for a specific reason. The fire service exists to serve people during a crisis. Due to the increasing demands on our profession I covered earlier in the book, fire departments across the country have been spending more time preparing for and training on things like hazardous material response and technical rescue. As a result, many departments find that they have less time to train on what one of our main focuses should be—structural firefighting. Perhaps your organization has faced similar challenges. One way for you, as a leader, to help your organization get back to the basics is by finding the proper tools to use as training props. In the fire service, legally acquiring abandoned buildings that can be used for various training evolutions is an incredibly valuable asset. In this section I provide tips to help firefighters do so. If acquiring buildings does not help you achieve your goal, perhaps the information in this section will help you begin to think about what your organization needs and offer some creative tips on how to attain it.

We can only learn so much by reading textbooks. Hands-on training presents us with an opportunity to physically practice techniques and sharpen skills. Reading about vertical ventilation and the best way to cut a hole in a roof is vastly different from pulling up to a training ground, positioning the apparatus, testing to make sure the saw will start, spotting and raising a ladder to the roof, climbing up, testing the roof, starting the saw again, and making the cut (fig. 3–25). This is the type of training firefighters can only receive at fire academies or by legally securing abandoned structures that are scheduled to be knocked down and obtaining permission to train in them.

By acquiring such a building, you'll have the opportunity to conduct hands-on drills in multiple areas, including vertical and horizontal ventilation, forcible entry, breaching walls, search and rescue, emergency bailout, firefighter rescue techniques, and in some cases flowing water. Having the opportunity to conduct these types of drills in a structure that you can take apart is priceless. Remember, this is why the fire service exists; therefore, leaders *must* acquire the appropriate tools to train on what they do the most (fig. 3–26).

It's not as difficult as you might think to find training tools, even ones as big as structures, to practice on. You just have to think outside the box. Begin by taking a moment to consider individuals or organizations within your community that may own and have access to structures within your area that are going to be knocked down, like the community building inspector, local contractors, or real estate investors.

If a member of my department takes the initiative to reach out to those individuals to inform them that our department is seeking structures for training and asks if they have any available, I would be impressed with that person's initiative. And as a leader, that individual would benefit by developing working relationships with valuable business contacts. You'll be surprised how many people are willing to work with their local fire department or any organization that is trying to improve its ability to serve others. If you don't have any leads, be creative. Talk with the head of your organization about placing an ad in paper stating that you are looking for a specific item for training purposes. Ask similar organizations that you don't compete with. For example, the police department may also find value in training in an abandoned structure, especially if it has special units like a SWAT team. This department may enthusiastically help you locate one.

Fig. 3–25. A firefighter can only learn so much by reading textbooks. Hands-on training presents an opportunity for firefighters to physically practice techniques and sharpen their skills.

Fig. 3–26. Abandoned buildings present firefighters with a valuable training opportunity. What tools could your organization benefit from attaining and training with?

The remainder of this section is written to provide leaders in the fire service with a guideline to follow once a structure is located. Again, you may not be looking to acquire a structure, but the information below may be useful in helping you plan and organize training evolutions that your organization needs.

Begin by getting permission in writing and taking all required legal actions before stepping foot on the property. Although a contractor or property owner may want to work with his or her local FD, no one wants to risk being sued if an injury occurs on his or her property. I am not an attorney, and I cannot tell you what your state, municipality, or department would require, but our department uses a very simple standard consent form drafted by our town attorney. The document we use is titled "Grant of Right to Use Premises for Fire Department Training." The document describes that an agreement has been made among the property owner, our department, and the municipality to use the property for training. It also explains that the licensee (which would be your department) will not claim any damages against the licensor (the property owner). We take this completed document, along with a copy of our certificate of insurance, and make sure all parties involved sign and receive copies before we proceed any further. Again, I encourage you to consult with your organization's legal representative to draft up a legal form granting permission to use these types of properties. A sample release form can be found in NFPA 1403, "Standard on Live Fire Training Evolutions."

Prior to training, be sure meet with the owners and discuss specific instructions they may have on any parts of the building that have salvage value or can't be harmed during the training. I once helped my department acquire a home with stained glass windows that the owner asked us to keep intact so they could be removed and reused. Some demolition companies often bid their services based on the salvage value of doors, windows, fixtures, and so on. There may also be landscape preservation issues. At one site, we had no choice but to place foot ladders in the middle of bushes in order to raise them to the second-floor window. By the end of the day, the bushes were destroyed. Luckily, the owners did not intend to salvage them; otherwise, we would have had some explaining to do since we only received permission to train "inside" the structure. This was clearly an oversight on my part. Make sure you discuss salvage issues with the owners so that everyone is on the same page before you begin.

The first building you acquire for training will be the most difficult, but once you establish a system, it will be well worth the effort. You may end up at the point where contractors call you when they acquire buildings to ask if your department would like to train in them before they knock them down or renovate them. With an established system in place, you can simply print out the necessary document for them to sign granting permission to train and review your previously developed lesson plans on topics that range from roof operations to basement fires.

Lesson plans: How to prepare for training evolutions

I'm a believer that if you want to get the most out of a training evolution you shouldn't begin on the training ground until you end on paper. In other words, write up a brief one-page lesson plan describing what type of drill you plan to conduct. In the lesson plan state your program objectives. This could be as simple as the following: "Drill topic: Breaching walls; Objective: To have each member breach a hole in the wall with an axe and/or Halligan and become proficient in the necessary skills for self-rescue and evacuation" (fig. 3–27).

Fig. 3–27. Kearny firefighters have legally acquired many abandoned structures to practice techniques like wall breaching.

Your next step should be to develop a list of safety precautions to take prior to beginning a drill. This can including checking the stairs for stability; inspecting the building for stability; making sure there are no wild animals or hazardous materials inside the structure; checking for mold, asbestos, and other environmental hazards; cleaning up debris; ensuring there are no hanging wires or broken glass lying around;

etc. You can find a sample checklist in NFPA 1403. The checklist also includes sections on live burn, permits, documents, notifications, insurance, building preparation, and course instructor and safety officer information. The preparation section provides essential reminders on what pre-drill steps to take and how to properly evaluate potential site hazards. Also describe who will be instructing the drill, what his or her credentials are, and who will be assigned as the safety officer. Once this is complete, it would be beneficial to send a notice to the members informing them of the upcoming drill. In the notice, describe the actual techniques that are going to be used, and reference what book or procedural guide the firefighters can review those techniques in. This will give all participants a chance to read up on the subject and come to the training site better prepared.

Prior to beginning the drill, have each participant sign and date a designated drill sign-in sheet. Have a binder designated to hold any lesson plans, permission forms, and sign-in sheets for training conducted in abandoned buildings. This will help with documentation and organization. Also conduct a walk-through of the structure and cover important safety tips prior to beginning. Any areas deemed unsafe should be secured and clearly marked, and instructors should make it clear that firefighters are to stay away from those areas.

In the week(s) before training begins, take all necessary safety precautions. In an abandoned structure that is scheduled for demolition, for example, confirm that the utilities have been shut off and the meter removed. Give each group a chance to train before you tear the building up. Be sure to save the destructive drills for later. Have a search and rescue drill before you start breaching walls and cutting holes in the roof. When training is complete, make sure the firefighters clean the area up as well as they can and resecure the building so that squatters cannot gain access into the property. If your department uses a marking system to alert emergency service personnel of an abandoned structure, be sure to follow your department SOP. After all is said and done, your members will have an opportunity to get rare hands-on training in areas they usually don't practice until actual incidents occur. This is a good time to bring them together and critique the exercises so you can discuss what you learned and determine the best way to accomplish the tasks when that time comes.

Fireproof Tip

A strong leader will work to acquire the right tools to ensure his or her organization has the chance to train in areas that are important to the overall success of the team. Doing so will provide you with a rare opportunity to practice skills that are necessary for success where it matters the most: in the field.

Technical Report Writing

Accurate and detailed report writing will always be an essential aspect of the emergency services. Currently, you may not have to write reports, but if you intend to be a leader, you absolutely will at some point.

In the emergency services profession, report writing is quite different from the corporate world, but in all cases, report writing requires a high level of professionalism. Leaders in the fire service cannot afford to slack when it comes to writing detailed reports, especially when we are talking about documenting what occurred at incidents. Although the fire service and law enforcement are both noble professions that are important to society, there are many differences between police and firefighters. Arguably, we provide better customer service. This is not a dig on police. Many of my best friends are uniformed police officers, and one of them brought this to my attention. The reason, he said, we provide better service is completely based on the nature of our jobs. When officers show up, someone is in danger of getting handcuffs put on; when we show up, we're greeted with smiles and someone is offering us a cup of coffee before we leave the scene. My friend also brought up another interesting difference between his profession and ours: "Your reports suck," he so eloquently said.

There is a reason that our profession has challenges when it comes to report writing. Police officers are trained to put the bad people away with good writing. They learn technical report writing skills in the academy. Fire academies don't teach these skills to new recruits. A firefighter may be on the job for years before ever being required to write a report.

Because of this, law enforcement is light-years ahead of us. This section may help bridge the gap.

I remember reading an actual report one time (not from a member of my department, thank goodness) that began with: "I've been on the job for many years. This was a bad fire, but we brought in a 1 ¾ " line and extinguished it without any problems." With the exception of starting out like a novel, this wasn't the worst report narrative introduction I have ever read. However, later in the report, the individual wrote: "Water supply was delayed because we couldn't get water from the hydrant." It went on to read: "We had difficult time finding the fire through thick smoke. Our air ran low, we had to retreat, replace our bottles before re-engaging." Then: "In the confusion, our crew was separated." And finally: "Another company put the fire out." I remember thinking, *Good thing you were able to extinguish the fire without any problems.*

What is the cause of poor report writing? This is usually attributed to one (or more) of these three reasons:

- Lack of training
- Lack of understanding what a good report consists of
- Poor writing skills

All three can be corrected with proper training, a good narrative format, and spell check (although for spell check to work, you have to get at least a few letters right).

One word can sum up why report writing is serious business: *liability*. Writing a detailed narrative report can be tedious, but it's necessary if you intend to fully protect yourself (and your organization). Narratives must be accurate and comprehensive. Inconsistent or incomplete reports create preventable liability. Don't ever lose sight of the fact that once you submit a report, you are locked into that document forever. Attempting to change (or contradicting) a report, can be considered highly suspicious. I constantly remind my officers of the following regarding reports: if you didn't write it down, it didn't happen!

We are most susceptible to liability when we are documenting low-frequency incidents such as those that involved fatalities, serious injuries, or major property damage (fig. 3–28).

Fig. 3–28. Major property damage leaves firefighters vulnerable to a potential lawsuit. A detailed report may help protect you and your organization.

Everything you document is public record. It can be used for you or against you. It's important to understand that reports are the *first* place lawyers look. I talked about several differences between police officers and firefighters. Now let me tell you the main difference between lawyers and firefighters: lawyers are smarter! Now, I don't necessarily agree with that, but consider this analogy. You may purchase 10 vehicles in your lifetime. You may do a week's worth of research, decide on the price you are willing to pay, and maybe you even get that price. Somehow, regardless of how much preparation you do, you still feel like you were taken for a ride. There is a reason why you feel this way. Even though you purchase 10 cars in your lifetime, the salesman you are dealing with sells 10 a day. The advantage goes to the house. The same thing can be said about lawyers. You may *know* you did the right thing at an incident, but lawyers know how to make you look incompetent. It's what they do. The key is to write an adequate and thorough report.

Even if you do everything right. you *cannot* assume that you or your organization will not get sued. Take the following example into consideration.

Your department responds to a working house fire and battles a tough blaze. Although the property suffered severe damage, the elderly woman who lived alone in the house was grateful for the hard-working members of your department that were able save some of her prized possessions. After the incident, you and two other firefighters are repacking the hose bed when another firefighter pulls out a camera and asks the three of you to stand together for a photo. You think nothing of it, and smile along with your buddies.

When you return to quarters, you quickly complete your report and enter it into the system so you can grab something to eat. The next day, the firefighter who took the picture posts it on a social network. You see the photo for the first time and realize that the three of you are smiling—with a damaged house in the background. Someone on the social network who sees the picture just happens to be the grandson of the woman who owns the house. He prints out the picture and shows it to her. Furious, the woman, who happened to lose her dog in the fire, brings the photo to an attorney and says, "I want to know why these firemen are having fun at my expense." Two days later, the attorney has your report on his desk. You suddenly regret not having written a more detailed report.

Reports are written for two reasons:

- To educate people who were not at the incident but who need to know details about what transpired, and

- To help you recall incident specifics months and years later.

Adequate reports consisting of detailed facts (not general information or opinion) will do more than just prove you did the right thing with a detailed narrative. It will also enable you to recall specifics five years after the incident. To be adequate, a report will include the *who*, *what*, *where*, *when*, *why*, and *how* of an incident. It will also be easy to understand and consistent with other reports that you have written. More important than anything else, reports should be able to defend themselves. In other words, if a lawyer looks at your report, you want her to think, "Looks like they did everything right."

To accomplish this goal, experts recommend that when writing narratives, such as the one needed for a structure fire report, firefighters use a well-crafted format. The format I designed for structure fire narratives has 11 simple headings. All I do is paste those headings into my reporting system and write a few sentences to describe what occurred. The headings are simply meant to jog my memory and help ensure I don't miss any key components. The following are the 11 areas, followed by a brief clarifying statement to help you understand what to mention in your report.

Structure Fire Format (with clarifying statements)

1. En route. (List any actions taken from the call until you arrive on scene.)

2. Establish command. (Explain whether you established or assumed command.)

3. Size-up factors. (Discuss what size-up factors influenced your decision making process.)

4. Initial radio report (IRR). (Describe any information you provided in your IRR that had an effect on the initial strategy and tactics or responding companies.)

5. Resources requested. (Provide a list of all resources that you requested at the fire and explain why.)

6. Incident Command System. (Describe the full extent of your implementation of the ICS.)

7. Strategies and tactics. (Describe the assignments that were given and the strategic objectives.)

8. Problems encountered. (List any problems encountered that you may not have already addressed.)

9. Under control. (Document the time the fire was reported under control and describe actions taken after declaring the fire under control.)

10. Transfer or termination of command. (Explain if you terminated or transferred command. If you transferred, to whom?)

11. Additional information. (Mention any additional information that you feel must be documented.)

You don't have to use my format, but I strongly encourage you to design your own. Doing so will allow for consistency. This method works with any type of report writing system in which you have to duplicate reports. For example, you may be expected to write a report summarizing your actions and accomplishments at the end of each workweek or month. It would benefit you to use a similar system.

Here are some additional helpful tips:

- Write your report when the incident is fresh in your mind.
- Spell out commonly abbreviated phrases such as company officer (CO).
- If your system allows it, compose in a word processing program then cut/paste into your reporting system.
- Use spell check (proofreader).
- Reread before submitting.
- Imagine that your entire report will be read in your absence in a meeting (such as a post-incident analysis).

The goal of a fire service professional can be summed up with four words: do your job right. The goal of a report can be summed up with two: prove it!

Fireproof Tip

Writing a detailed narrative report can be tedious, but it's necessary if you intend to fully protect yourself and your organization. To ensure consistency, use a format or template as a guide. This will also help jog your memory and help ensure you don't miss any key components. Remember, if you didn't write it down, it didn't happen.

Leadership on the Fireground

When it comes to officers, there is a vast difference between leading in the firehouse and leading on the fireground. The day I became a firefighter, I was told that the fire service is a paramilitary style of organization. Without question there are similarities, specifically the structure of rank, splendor of dress, and sternness of discipline. There is also the structure of command on the fireground. As much as those things resemble the traditions of the military, there is one huge distinguishing component that makes our organization different from the military: labor unions.

There are few organizations in the world that have to combine the different philosophies that leaders implement to effectively manage unions and paramilitary organizations. The fire service is one of them. Many times, the greatest challenge a fire service leader will encounter is acknowledging this fact. The next greatest challenge would be to develop the skills that are needed to lead in both areas.

The information provided prior to this section will serve you well as a leader around the fire station. However, it's difficult to deny the fact that the goals of the organization will not always match the goals of the labor union. This is one of the reasons it is helpful to get others to participate as often as possible. When the members of a union help formulate ideas, strategies, and goals, you are less likely to encounter resistance. They are more likely to buy into ideas they help create. Union heads want to know that the organizational leaders are listening to their members' feedback. The paramilitary model, on the other hand, has often been criticized for being inflexible and unnecessary. Perhaps around quarters and in corporate America this thought holds some weight; on the fireground is another story altogether.

In the thick of battle, firefighters respond well to a leader who can rapidly assess situations, formulate strategic plans, make accurate decisions, and calmly give out assignments. As a leader, when you can attach purpose to the assignment, others will trust and value your capabilities on the fireground (fig. 3–29). The management style outlined in the previous sections of this chapter work well, but the rapidly changing fireground is not the place to ask for subordinate input (fig. 3–30). There will be times when input is necessary. There will also be times when it is encouraged, such as when someone recognizes an unsafe condition that has been overlooked; otherwise, involving too many people when formulating a strategic plan can be counterproductive and costly. This should be done in the preplanning stage.

Fig. 3–29. Firefighters respond well to strong fireground leaders who delegate tasks that have purpose.

Fig. 3–30. The rapidly changing fireground is not the place to ask for subordinate input.

Step Up and Lead

Emergency scenes run most smoothly when they are managed with similar philosophies that are used by the military when engaged in battle. This is where the Incident Command System and National Incident Management System (NIMS) become vital. These systems enable fire service leaders to organize an incident by incorporating military aspects of leadership at the fire scene. Once the incident is complete, a leader can take off the general's cap and go back to managing in more balanced way, as described previously. Fire service leaders who run their shift or department as if they are on the fireground at all times are missing one key point. The majority of the time they (and their crew) are in uniform will be spent around the station, on the training ground, or responding to routine calls. A person absolutely must show leadership qualities in these areas to earn the respect of members. Trying to earn respect on the fireground without being able to do so around the firehouse can be a difficult task for any leader.

Fireproof Tip

The fireground should be managed with similar philosophies that are used by our military when engaged in battle. This is where the Incident Command System and NIMS become vital; however, leadership on the fireground is different than leadership in the fire station. Don't lose sight of the fact that the majority of time you spend in your uniform will be around the firehouse, on the training ground, and responding to routine calls. If you do not show the qualities of a leader in these three places, you will find it difficult to lead when it counts the most. If you do show strength in these three areas, you are ready to *step up and lead*!

4

CUSTOMER SERVICE

Culture

Every organization has a culture. It is created either by design or default. Creating a culture of customer service does not happen by accident. Buying into the concept of layered leadership (the need for leaders throughout an entire organization) is especially important when it comes to customer service.

Since the day I became a Kearny firefighter, there has always been a select group of firefighters at various ranks who have gone above and beyond when it comes to serving the public. They are individuals with big hearts, and they have done a tremendous job representing our department. Any time they show up in a T-shirt with our department logo, they understand that they are selflessly donating their time to do something that is ultimately going to make our organization shine. They don't do it for fame, and they certainly don't do it for fortune. They do it because they have big hearts and giving natures. A smart leader will recognize that anytime a person representing an organization does something good, it makes that organization shine.

Some of the events our members have worked to develop, enhanced, and donated their time for include community picnics, public education seminars, literacy groups, junior police academy, drug awareness–related events where we performed extrication demonstrations (fig. 4–1), and fund raisers for organizations or individuals in need of community support. A handful of our members, led by a dedicated firefighter named Tom Atwell, even traveled to other states to help brothers and sisters from across the country rebuild their homes after natural disasters such as Hurricane Katrina. After Superstorm Sandy decimated the Jersey Shore, Atwell and a team of firefighters (too many to mention) started a relief effort. They entered water-damaged communities and went from home to home helping people gut their houses to prepare to rebuild. These men and women, like most in the fire service, understand that they are in the business of customer service, and in our industry, that means never losing sight of the fact that most of the people we encounter are in the midst of a crisis.

Fig. 4–1. Firefighters perform a mock extrication for high school students to warn against the dangers of texting and driving and/or driving under the influence of drugs or alcohol.

Helping others seems to be part of the DNA of most firefighters. Creating culture, however, goes beyond just being a good person. There has to be a clear and focused objective or mission on behalf of your organization. Like any mission, it starts with the vision of one person—a leader. In this case, that one person can be you. Once others see what you are striving to accomplish, and they understand that it will have a tremendously positive impact on your organization and buy into that vision, you are well on your way to creating a culture by design rather than default.

Everyone plays a role in creating culture, from the person who answers the phones to the leaders in the field. But the individuals who have the greatest impact on the organization overall are usually those at the top of an organization.

Fire officers play critical roles in creating the right customer service culture within the fire service. Officers have the obligation to set the standard, which can be accomplished by taking the following actions:

- Provide leadership and guidance on what is acceptable and what is not.

- Set a good example for others to learn from.

- Clearly communicate the mission of the organization.

- Support the field members who are in daily contact with the customers.

- Publicly recognize outstanding effort and make a big deal out of the right activity.

Once again, true to human nature, this is usually where some individuals will point out that the people at the top of their organization may not be doing any of the actions listed here. Why do we do this? I believe it's because too many people look for someone to blame when things aren't perfect. If you just fell into that trap, now is a great time to remember that *you* can make the difference. You can help your organization achieve the right results and begin to create the right kind of culture.

Remember, the right activity *always* produces the right result. The right result for any service-based organization is providing the best customer care possible. To do this, remember the acronym Customer-KARE.

- **Knowledge.** It cannot be emphasized enough that you must understand how to do your job and how to meet your customers' expectations.

- **Attitude.** The manner in which you approach and interact with others will have a lasting effect. People always remember how you made them feel.

- **Respect.** Respect your customers; otherwise your organization is destined to fail. Don't ever forget, the customer is always right.

- **Excellence.** This should be what you want to come to the minds of people when they think about and talk about the experience they had with you and your organization.

If the upper management of an organization fails to recognize the importance of providing great service to their customers, the organization is heading for failure. That is, unless the individuals who are dealing directly with the customers (like you) "get it!"

Who are the customers?

Anyone who interacts with your organization, on any level, is a customer.

It's been said that in the fire service we are constantly meeting new people and spending the worst moments of their life with them. When a person is having one of the worst moments of his or her life, firefighters need to have one of the best moments of their life. That is why fire departments exist. Fighting a house fire or cutting people out of cars may be the first image that comes to most people minds when they think of firefighters, but our profession is much more than that. There are so many ways to help the public, and some are so simple that often they are overlooked, such as the ones outlined earlier in this section. My first bit of advice is to make the decision that you are going to exceed expectations.

High-quality customer service is the key to exceeding expectations, and exceeding expectations is the key to your organization's survival (fig. 4–2).

That sentence stands alone for a reason. If you haven't taken time to think about the importance or customer service, you don't fully understand what your purpose is. In short, your purpose is to find a need and fill it.

Fig. 4–2. High-quality customer service is the key to exceeding expectations.

Finding a need in the fire service is not a difficult thing to do. When a person calls and says, "Help, my house is on fire!" the need is obvious. Our job is to get there as fast as possible and fulfill the oath we took to save lives and property and protect the weak.

To ensure we don't get ahead of ourselves, let's cover two basic things—the definition of customer service and the goal you and your organization should strive for.

The definition of customer service: an organization's ability to supply its customers' wants and needs.

The goal of your organization: to provide the highest level of service to your customers and to enhance the image of your organization to gain public support.

This goal should be the minimum. A true leader knows we must exceed the expectations of our customers. In our profession, people who call on us need—among other things—someone to help, a timely response, courtesy, a solution to their problem, and empathy. What would happen if we took it one step further and provided them with service beyond what they expected?

In 2012, I attended the Fire Department Instructors Conference (FDIC) in Indianapolis, Indiana. I was honored to be chosen to speak on the topic of fireground command at what is arguably the largest fire conference in the world. That year, there were close to 30,000 FDIC attendees. The day before my class, I walked to my assigned classroom to get a feel for it and familiarize myself with the layout. I was lucky enough to walk in on another class that was in session. The instructor was none other than Chief Alan Brunacini of the Phoenix Fire Department, the 2006 Career Fire Chief of the Year (fig. 4–3). *Fire Chief* magazine described Chief Brunacini as a man who uses words like simple, basic, and common-sense, a man who is to the fire service what W. Edwards Deming was to manufacturing. As a fire service leader, he didn't micromanage, he gave credit where credit was due, and he learned his management philosophy at his mother's knee. Chief Brunacini will always be considered one of the legendary fire chiefs who have had an impact on the American fire service. Needless to say, I immediately took my seat in the back and listened intently as Chief Brunacini spoke about customer service.

Fig. 4–3. Chief Alan Brunacini speaking to a group of firefighters about the importance of exceeding the expectations of our customers.

Chief Brunacini was talking about the day members of his department responded to a dryer fire. The incident was minimized by a quick response by the FD, but the woman who lived there called Chief Brunacini to tell him how pleased she was with the service the fire department provided. What stood out for her was how one firefighter took the clothes out of the dryer and neatly folded and placed them in a dry place. Chief Brunacini went on to say that he was pleased with this action and went to the fire station to talk with the member. Ironically, the firefighter was folding towels when he walked in to see him.

I learned two major lessons from this brief story that Chief Brunacini told the audience: (1) The thought that went in to this level of service from a firefighter was exceptional (he *stepped up*), and (2) Chief Brunacini was classy enough to praise the individual and express his appreciation, which surely had a positive impact.

Chief Brunacini's methods are legendary in the fire service. His former officers have said they valued the fact that he let them take ownership of projects and that he never took credit. He once said:

> I think people in an organization begin to believe and trust in that organization the moment you let them own their own part of the organization. The more we cut them out of that and move away from that, then you have people that mistrust each other, and pretty soon there are secret meetings. You have an elite group of people who are managing an organization. They're making deals, and everything is a secret in that organization. I wouldn't want to go into a fire with that environment in the work group that you depended on to either live or die on. Do you trust the organization and the people who run it? It's not very complicated.

As far as customer service goes, in my personal opinion, Chief Brunacini raised the bar for the fire service. He helped many departments develop some form of a customer service model by introducing and applying the elements outlined below. Take a moment to consider how this simple model could benefit your organization when dealing with customers.

Customer service model

- Always be nice.

- Always provide the best possible service to customers.

- Regard everyone you come in contact with as a customer.

- Treat people the way you would want others to treat you (or your family).

- Don't disqualify the customer with your personal qualifications.

- Consider how what you are doing looks to others.

- Always work on improving your organization's customer service.

- Everyone in the organization plays a part (and is responsible for his or her behavior).

- Don't ever forget, to the customer, you are your organization.

The Golden Rule

If you are not familiar with the golden rule of customer service, here it is: the customer is always right!

Yes, always, even when customers are wrong, you have to find a way to let them feel as if they are right. There are members of the fire service who roll their eyes at this one. They say things like, "If a customer is yelling at me because there is a hole in the roof, and we had to do this to ventilate so we could search for life and fire, how is the customer right?"

Let me explain. Even if your actions were correct, when it comes to the way someone feels . . . that person is right. When someone says she is cold, even though you are sweating, she's right—because she is cold. You can spend 30 minutes arguing with her that she is wrong, it's 90° outside, her air conditioning is not working, and so she can't be cold, but if she says she is cold, you are wasting your time. When it comes to customer service, great organizations teach their people to understand that it's more important be polite than it is to be right.

In the fire service, a great way to deal with upset customers after damaging their house is to use a variation of the well-known *feel, felt, found* technique. In sales, when a person says, "It's too expensive," seasoned sales professionals may respond by saying something like, "I know how you *feel*—I *felt* the same way before I began using this product, but let me share with you what I *found* out . . ." They would then go on to explain the many benefits that result from using a specific product or service and how the rewards far outweigh the cost.

As a fire chief, I use the *feel, felt, why* technique. When a person comes up to me and complains that we had broken his windows (fig. 4–4), I begin by saying, "I understand how you *feel*—I would have *felt* the same way before I became a firefighter, but let me explain *why* we had to do this . . ." I then go on to explain why ventilation is needed to help save life and property.

Fig. 4–4. When a customer is upset about the damage our members did to his home, it's a leader's responsibility to take time to explain why this damage occurred.

I don't argue or tell the person he or she is wrong for feeling that way. I agree with them: *"I understand how you feel,"* then I validate their feelings: *"I would have felt the same way before I became a firefighter,"* then I educate them is a non-confrontational manner, *"Let me explain why we had to do this."*

Turn of the Tide

Anyone who thinks respect comes automatically for the men and women wearing a fire department uniform because of the nature of our work could not be more wrong. Although there may have been a time where this was true, times have changed. At least they have for career firefighters.

Fewer than 10 years after 9/11, it seemed as though the majority of politicians turned their backs on the fire service. After our government bailed out the banking and auto industries, they began to put pressure on local politicians to find "creative ways" to balance their budgets. The country was in the midst of a financial crisis, and politicians from all parties began to look at career firefighters as part of the problem. Their message was, "The good, hardworking citizens and taxpayers can no longer afford to pay for the high salaries and rich benefits of firefighters." Mitt Romney had accepted the Republican nomination to run for president, and he was taking a page right out of New Jersey Governor Chris Christie's playbook. That message included the following plan for municipalities to balance their budgets: fewer firefighters, fewer police officers, and fewer teachers.

Now, I'm not making a political point or trying to express my personal views about politics. I'm just stating the facts. During this time, career firefighters were being beaten up by both parties. Firefighters seemed to have gone from heroes to zeroes in the blink of an eye. Non-firefighters reading this book cannot imagine how it felt to hear people on the radio, out in public, and even at family events talking about how unfair it was that career firefighters had a pension and good health benefits in such a struggling economy (fig. 4–5). Ten years earlier, friends of mine scoffed at the idea of becoming a firefighter because the pay was so low. Suddenly, those same friends were scoffing at the reality that our incomes were not being reduced the way theirs were because we had a contract. After a turn in the economy, the shoe was on the other foot, and all of a sudden many people felt we were compensated too much. Any person or organization that has had a portion of the public turn against them would understand how challenging these times could be.

Fig. 4–5. Many people felt we were compensated too much during the down economy.

One day, we were conducting an elaborate technical rescue drill at an asphalt manufacturing facility in our community. It was about 90 degrees and our members were standing on top of a 35,000-gallon tank wearing full personal protective equipment. Some members were being lowered into the sweltering hot tank, packaging a 160-pound manikin, and raising it back to the top. Three hours into the exercise, our members were soaked with sweat and physically exhausted. I decided to take a ride to a local deli to pick up some iced teas for the crew. While in line, I was standing behind an elderly woman and a man. They weren't together, but they knew each other. At the time, our salaries had been published in the local newspaper and there was talk of layoffs and pay freezes. We had started a multimedia campaign to gain public support. The campaign included articles in local papers, interviews on local television programs and radio stations, and a flyer that was mailed to every resident in our community. The flyer informed residents about the threat we were up against and outlined all the services we perform for our community. We were doing well with that effort. However, not everyone understood the complexities and scope of our job duties. What I experienced that afternoon in the deli proved it.

"I called the mayor," the woman said.

"Really, about what?" the man asked.

"I told him my taxes are too high," she continued. "If something doesn't change, I am going to have to move out of this town."

"It's the same everywhere. Where are you going to go?" he asked.

"I don't know, anywhere, I just can't afford to live here anymore."

Without looking at me, the man pointed in my direction and said, "These guys are the problem."

He was referring to our salaries. Obviously, I wanted to defend our profession, but he was a local resident, and I was well aware that he had just received a flyer in his mailbox that outlined all the services we perform for the community. He was simply not a fan, and it was clear to me that confronting him would have been pointless and unprofessional. Since he didn't have the courage to look at me when he made his comment, I felt the best option would be for me to ignore it altogether. If I had said something, he probably would have just walked out of the deli, called the mayor, and said he had a confrontation with a firefighter. I felt it would be better to live to fight another day. I only wished the man could see what my crew was doing at that very moment.

The reason I tell this story is to share with you that just because *you* know how hard you work and understand the sacrifices that you are willing to make doesn't mean *others* know. There will be times when you need to address an issue, and there are other times when you should just let it go.

The lesson I learned that day was that, for the first time in the history of our organization, we had to wonder if people supported us or not. Instead of spending my time and energy contemplating who stood with us and who stood against us, the only thing we could do is *step up*. The goal my crew set was simple. Every time we come in contact with civilians, we will smile (when appropriate), be kind, and treat them with the respect they deserve. There is no question, this has been our focus since the beginning, but providing exceptional customer service was more important now than ever before.

Although it is true that respect is earned, not given, there is a caveat. You will never earn respect from others if you don't give it to them first. This is the approach you should take with your customers.

"You will never earn respect from others if you don't give it to them first."

The man in the deli didn't want to hear that we were riding with three-member engine companies instead of four. He didn't care that we closed a company or took pay freezes, or about the challenges we had been dealing with due to high turnover rates and the loss of knowledgeable veterans. You may be dealing with similar people. This doesn't mean you shouldn't work to educate civilians and politicians about the challenges your organization is faced with, but there is an absolute right and wrong way to do so. I believe that all firefighters, especially new ones, need to be taught how to deal with negative comments and confrontations with civilians.

During difficult times like the one I just described, it takes a leader to institute a concentrated and deliberate attempt to be as professional as possible. In today's fire service, every member in every department is expected to operate and behave professionally at all times. It's essential that we teach firefighters how to direct questions to their superiors and how to treat customers as their top priority.

When dealing with the public, firefighters must be educated on the importance of looking professional, controlling their emotions and attempts at humor, and projecting confidence. It is critical that every member of the fire service is taught how to interact with the public (fig. 4–6).

Fig. 4–6. Firefighters must always deal with customers in a professional manner.

There are seven simple actions we teach newer firefighters when dealing with customers.

1. Be friendly.

2. Make eye contact.

3. Give your full attention.

4. Say please and thank you.

5. Address adults as ma'am or sir.

6. Avoid confrontation.

7. Direct people with questions to your supervisor.

Although the following questions go beyond just interacting with customers, a leader should also educate team members on ethical behavior. Before participating in an activity or taking action while representing an organization, teach others to ask themselves these four questions:

- Is it legal, moral, and ethical?
- Is it at my level of expertise/training?
- Does it align with the overall mission of my organization?
- Is it something my family would be proud of?

Whenever a firefighter begins to show signs of frustration about our profession, it's the leader's job to remind him or her why we exist. When tragedy strikes, we are there to make things better. Most of the time we may feel insignificant, but when the alarm sounds, we are about to become the most important team of professionals in the world to one or more people. I believe we should never lose sight of that fact. A leader should always remind others on the team how important they are.

....

"It is not the employer who pays the wages.

Employers only handle the money.

It is the customer who pays the wages."

—Henry Ford

....

Leaders understand that a high level of appreciation needs to be shown any time their organization comes in contact with the public. That big fire engine full of tools we ride around in, the fire station we call home more than 40 hours a week, and the paycheck we get for doing the greatest job on earth all came from somewhere. Firefighters should never forget who paid the millions of dollars needed to start and sustain a fire department . . . taxpayers!

In return for making it possible for us to serve the public, our customers need to know they can rest their head at night and their families are safe because they know beyond a shadow of a doubt we are going to be there when they need us with unconditional support— meaning without judgment.

Once that type of trust is earned between an organization and its customers, it should never be taken for granted. The best way for firefighters to show their appreciation is by providing the highest level of customer service they possibly can. We do this by going above and beyond.

When a father of two young children hears a pop in his basement and smells a strange burning odor late in the evening, he calls the fire department. When we tell him it's safe to go back to sleep, he doesn't argue. It doesn't matter how sure he was that something had gone wrong 15 minutes earlier. When we check it out and say there's no problem, he breathes a sigh of relief and thanks us for coming. That is an amazing level of trust and respect we are receiving from a stranger (fig. 4–7).

Fig. 4–7. People trust us with the lives of their children when we tell them their home is safe and they can go back to sleep. We have an obligation to respect them by being professional and thorough.

It's the same level of trust and respect we receive when we respond on a medical call to assist an elderly woman who is weak from battling an illness. She and her husband may have been high school sweethearts, married for more than 50 years. She is everything in the world to him, yet he trusts us to care for her without question. It's our obligation to honor that level of respect with an equal level of respect.

I'm grateful that the men and women on my department understand the importance of providing great customer service. If you work for an organization that does not "get it," don't make the mistake of blaming the newest members of your team. It's your responsibility to educate them. I say *your* responsibility because you are the one reading this book. You get it! Become the change you want to see in your organization and others will follow your lead. I promise.

Personal Development

Everything we do from the moment we walk into the firehouse until our shift ends has the potential of liability. Not training our people would create an even greater liability threat. Although you can never prevent liability 100%, you have a greater chance of doing so if you and all the members of your organization are properly trained.

Fire departments, like every other organization, owe it to their customers to train every day. I'm not just talking about fireground training. On that topic, I'll just say this: if a crew is spending more time on the fireground than on the training ground, they are not training enough, period.

The type of training I'm talking about is on topics such as the ones outlined in this book or in books like *Pride and Ownership*. I am always impressed when I see a firefighter reading a book like *How to Win Friends and Influence People*. Anyone who scoffs at the idea hasn't learned this one incredible lesson: the majority of the problems you will have in life will be a direct result of ineffective or poor people skills.

In order to improve, you must work on developing in areas where you are lacking. When it comes to customer service, the goal is to develop your social abilities.

....

"The majority of problems you will have in life will be a direct result of ineffective or poor people skills."

....

Tactically, there is always a possibility that a firefighter's actions can be questioned. In the ever-changing world of the fireground, things happen quickly and are often unpredictable. Although we can control our actions, there are thousands of factors we cannot control, such as how many victims are in a structure, how long it will take to get three-alarm staffing at the scene, or what type of contents are on fire. What we do have control over is how we communicate with our customers. Learning how to deal with people in a professional manner is essential for your personal success. Training the other members of your organization to do the same is critical to the success of your overall organization.

What can one person do?

To begin with, you can *only* do the right thing if your values are intact. When you hear a coworker saying something inappropriate, do you play along, or do you address it? Have you ever sat quietly and listened to a member of your organization make a demeaning remark about the organization or another member? Did you fail to speak up? Are you in a leadership position, but you don't like to discipline others because you didn't want to be the bad guy? Do you fail to speak up when someone performs an unsafe act (fig. 4–8)? This ultimately leads to a breakdown in performance, which will make others question your motives, which will eventually translate to poor customer service and possible litigation.

It is important to step up and do your part to help create a positive public image for your organization. Those who work on developing themselves seem to be the ones who have a better grasp on how to deal with others. The key to personal development is education. When you read the right books, attend the right seminars, and associate with the right people directly or through audio recordings or videos, you are heading in the right direction.

Fig. 4–8. If you see or hear someone doing something unsafe on the fireground, speak up. The same thing can be said when you see or hear someone acting inappropriately.

The actions of one single firefighter can affect the overall public's opinion of all firefighters—and the organization that individual works for. Without question, the majority of fire chiefs receive more phone calls about firefighters acting inappropriately than when they act professionally. This isn't as much a reflection of poor customer service as it is a statement about human nature. People call to complain; they rarely call when they are pleased. Consider the "How am I driving?" bumper stickers that can be seen on back of many commercial vehicles. If the person is following local traffic laws, using his blinker properly, and pausing so pedestrians can cross, do you think someone is going to call the number on the sticker and say, "I just want to tell you how great a job your driver is doing"?

There are only a few actions on the driver's part that would cause a person to make that call. The first, by an overwhelming majority, is reckless driving. The second would be if someone witnessed an incredibly generous act on behalf of the driver. For example, if the driver witnessed an elderly woman drop two bags of groceries and pulled over to help her pick them up. There is a possibility—albeit small—that someone might make a phone call to report such a kind act.

Take it upon yourself to set the example for others and work hard to develop your ability to communicate at a higher level with your customers. Help educate your organization on how to act appropriately. When members of your organization act inappropriately, it takes a strong leader to immediately correct their behavior and educate those people on the importance of preserving a good public image. Once again, it all comes down to leading *you* first.

The First Impression

There is absolutely no doubt in my mind that every organization wants what we have in the fire service—*respect* from the people we serve (fig. 4–9).

It will benefit any leader to understand that it's not about you, your company, or your services. It's about your ability to meet your customers' needs and add value to their lives. I am amazed by how many companies in the U.S. don't listen to their customers. They spend more time talking about their revenue problems than their customers' needs. If they would start paying more attention to their customers' needs, they would no longer have a revenue problem. The fire service is different. The word *service* is the key to our profession. A great leader will understand this and instill this mind set within others.

Creating or expanding business relationships is not about selling—it's about establishing trust, rapport, and value creation without selling. Call me crazy, but I don't want to talk to someone who wants to manage my account, develop my business, or engineer my sale. I want to communicate with someone. I want to communicate with someone who knows the names of my children and asks about them whenever we talk. Until then, all they care about is getting my money. At least, that's the way I look at it.

Fig. 4–9. The fire service has *earned* the respect of the public. Has your organization?

When people call 9-1-1, they expect to talk with a person and be treated with respect and prompt service. They have a very important need that must be addressed immediately. Anything less would be unacceptable for the customer and the organization. Too many organizations fail to realize this. When a single mother with two kids calls her cable company because her service went out, she doesn't want to listen to an automated machine directing her through a series of prompts that the CEO of Microsoft would have a difficult time navigating his way through.

No one wants to be greeted with a message stating that his or her call might be recorded for training purposes. Although we don't state it, every emergency call that comes in is recorded. I'm sure you have watched the news once or twice when they reported a story about an emergency dispatcher treating a caller in an unprofessional manner. The story always includes a portion of the recording of the call. It's beyond me how a 9-1-1 operator can be callous and disrespectful, but it does happen. And when it does, someone gets fired.

The people answering the phones must understand how important they are to your organization. When a person in distress calls, the dispatchers are our first impression. Corporate America has been trying to stress this point for years. The receptionist at a Fortune 500 company, for example, will be the first—and sometimes only—person a caller will talk with when she needs a problem solved. I'm baffled every time I make a call to a large corporation and get an automated message. That tells me I'm just a number. Don't try to solve my problem by making me give you my personal information and press a dozen numbers before my call is directed to the office it needs to get to. Give me a person, ask me what's wrong, then send me to the person who can solve my problem.

Can you imagine calling 9-1-1 and hearing: press 1 for fire; press 2 for vehicle accident; press 3 for chemical spill; press 4 for difficulty breathing; press 5 for . . . you get the point. We are lucky that we have—and God willing, always will have—an actual human being answering the call. Now, we need to make sure our dispatchers realize two things:

- How important they are, and
- How to do their job correctly.

Dispatchers are ambassadors of the emergency services and they must *step up and lead* every time they answer a call. The same can be said about every member of your organization who deals with a customer on any level. You will have plenty of opportunities to be the first impression someone has when it comes to your organization. Always be courteous and professional. Understand that you may be the only person the customer will associate with your organization. It doesn't matter if you are speaking with a 9-year-old child or an 80-year-old senior, never be unprofessional, appear disconnected, or act rude to the customer. With that in mind, the same question should be on the forefront of your mind every time you are dealing with a customer, and that question is, "How may I help you?"

The Lifeblood of Your Organization

What is the purpose of your organization's existence? Have you ever given much thought to the bottom line reason why your team exists? If you intend to lead, you must be able to summarize your mission in just a few words. By now, you know the lifeblood of the profession of firefighting and can sum it up in two words: customer service.

Yes, we run into burning buildings and hang from skyscrapers on ropes to save people, but it's more than that. Overall, the public has been impressed with three things that the fire service provides: rapid response, professionalism, *and* kind and caring service. Those three things would serve any organization well.

I had been working as the training captain for a little more than a year when my chief called me into his office. As I walked in, he was sitting behind his desk and a woman in her mid-30s was sitting opposite him. She had tears in her eyes.

"I'd like to introduce you to Captain Viscuso," the chief said, "He is going to help make this happen. Please tell him what you told me."

I shook her hand and sat down next to her. I didn't know what to expect.

"My 11-year-old daughter, Angelina, has been battling brain cancer," she said, trying her best to hold back her emotions. I was doing the same. The woman continued, "She was terrified to begin radiation therapy. After six weeks, she began chemo treatments, which lasted for 15 months. To try and keep her positive, I asked her what she would want after she completed her treatments. She told me that all she wanted was a ride on a fire engine."

My eyes welled up. I knew of the girl. At least once a week our guys were called out to help carry Angelina from her home to the car or vice versa as she went to or returned from the hospital for treatments. I remained silent as the woman continued. She looked as if she was expecting to be let down. "Angelina just finished her treatments. There were many times where she suffered from pain and sickness, but we kept reminding her that she was going to get her ride on the fire engine when this was all over. Is there any way possible she could get a ride or maybe just sit on a fire engine for a few seconds?"

"Of course," I said. "When would you like to do this?"

A massive smile appeared on her face, "Would sometime next week be okay?"

We set a date and exchanged information. I shook the woman's hand again. She left to go and tell her daughter the good news. That night

I was lying in bed, thinking about this little girl. Of all the things she could have asked for, she wanted a ride in a fire engine. How could that be? After what she's been through, she deserves so much more. I got out of bed, turned on my computer, and searched for a similar story I remembered reading about a child who was dying of leukemia. His wish was to be a firefighter. I found it under the title, "Am I a Fireman Yet?" If you haven't read the story, I encourage you to do so. It can easily be found online. I printed it out and made several copies.

The next evening, I attended an awards ceremony for local emergency service members. I placed one copy of the story on each table. Throughout the night, I watched as several firefighter and emergency service professionals read the story. As I expected, few were able to read it without shedding a tear.

After awards were given out to various people, I was brought up to say a few words. I referenced the document and asked people to raise their hands if they read it. Almost everyone in the room had. I then told them about Angelina's wish. I said, "Instead of giving her a ride on a fire engine, why don't we give her a parade?" When I asked if anyone would like to participate as we celebrate this little girl's life, nearly every hand in the room was raised. The next day, I typed up a document titled "Angelina's Parade" and sent it out to the people who attended the ceremony. As you can imagine, many of those people forwarded the document to other local police, fire, and EMS organizations. The local paper got wind of what was about to happen and wrote a quick blurb about it.

I called Angelina's mother and told her what had transpired and advised her to have her daughter in front of the house at a certain time of day, but not to be surprised at what comes around the corner. I'm sure in her mind, she expected to see one fire engine with lights and sirens, but we had a much bigger plan.

On the day of the ride, at 1:30 p.m., more than 100 residents arrived in front of Angelina's house sporting signs to show their support for the young girl. The sounds of sirens grew louder and louder when finally, around the corner came an engine with a banner in front reading "Angelina's Parade." Directly behind the engine was the Kearny Fire Department marching band, followed by nine more engines, two ambulances, a paramedic, two police vehicles, a Port Authority rescue truck, the Blue Knights law enforcements motorcycle club of New Jersey, souped-up vintage cars, a bagpiper, and a bunch of people dressed in cartoon character suits. Several television crews and reporters also came to cover the event (fig. 4–10).

Fig. 4–10. Angelina's Parade was a reminder to us all that we are a customer service-based organization first and foremost.

When we reached the house, two of our members carried Angelina from her front porch to the lead fire engine. Her parade traveled twice around the block. Then the engine took her for a ride around town. It was an awesome sight to see. A few days after the news aired the event on local television, I received a phone call from a man who worked for a record company. He said he was moved by the event. He told me that he read in one of the articles that Angelina loved Christina Aguilera. As it turned out, this man worked for the company that was currently producing Christina Aguilera's latest album. He said she was going to be in the studio next week and wanted to know if I could get him in contact with Angelina's parents so he could invite the family down.

The next thing I know, Angelina was in the studio with her favorite recording artist.

Although it was not our intention for the fire department to gain community notoriety, the actions of our members made everyone in town realize that we weren't just there to answer distress calls, we were there to serve in any way possible. An event like the one we organized could never have happened without a number of individuals stepping up.

Every leader needs to understand that the purpose of his or her team's existence is the same: to serve. When you stop providing value to your customers, you lose sight of the very thing that matters the most. I love Gary Vaynerchuk's book *Crush It*. Chapter 9 is titled "The Best Marketing Strategy Ever." The chapter consists of only one word: *care*.

Your success in *any* business will always be in direct proportion to your ability to care about your customers and exceed their expectations.

··

"Spend a lot of time talking to your customers face to face. Ask questions and listen. You'd be amazed how many people, companies, and organizations don't listen to their customers."

··

Pursue Excellence

Providing excellent customer service is a terrific goal and will bring your organization many benefits. You will be known for your professionalism and ability to turn negatives into positives. You will create a positive public image within your supportive community, the media, and (in the fire service's case) the governing body of your munici-pality. You will also have the advantage of keeping the chief off your back. All of these benefits will help improve the overall morale of your organization. There is no shortage of advantages to providing the best service possible.

Great service is not always defined by the outcome of the job. We may save the structure and a dozen pets because we located, confined, and extinguished a fire in record time, but if we caused a massive flood in the basement because we used an unnecessary amount of water, we may have an unhappy customer. That's just the way it goes sometimes.

I once heard a firefighter I respect say something that bothered me. He said, "When the building is on fire, we show up. That's all the customer service we need." Although I get his point, I completely disagree with it, and deep down inside, I think he disagrees with it as well. The fact is we have to psych ourselves up to get to the scene and get in the building. That's where the bravado part comes in. We don't know what we are responding to, and we can't afford to be afraid. In our profession, fear causes hesitation, and hesitation can result in disaster. With that said, firefighters have a responsibility to work on boosting their image with the public while still getting the job done.

I speak to fire departments throughout the country about the endless number of opportunities to provide exceptional customer service. If an organization responds to 6,000 calls a year, that's 6,000 opportunities to pursue excellence. Then there are the tens of thousands of other times firefighters interact with the public on a variety of levels. We can't just show up. We have to shine.

It's important that we try to manually open doors and windows before we pry them open and damage them. It's important that we show compassion toward the victims of fire or other tragedies, that we check carbon monoxide levels before letting occupants return to a structure, and that we secure buildings if occupants cannot reenter so that their possessions are safe. It's smart to take time to meet with local business owners and developers to tour their facilities and/or review their plans and provide feedback that will enable us to provide the best service possible (fig. 4–11). This is called excellent customer service, and it comes with great benefits.

Fig. 4–11. A firefighter assists a real estate developer with issues concerning water supply.

The following are ways in which excellent customer service will benefit you and your organization:

- You will be known for your professionalism.
- You will develop a reputation for being able to turn negatives into positives.
- You will create a positive public image within your community, the media, and politicians.
- You will gain community support.
- You will improve the morale of your organization.
- You will satisfy your customers, which will keep the boss off your back.

On the other hand, poor customer service also produces results—but not the type of results you'd like.

The following are ways in which poor customer service affects your organization:

- You will produce negative press, which may lead to political issues and lack of support from the public.

- You will increase the possibility of legal issues.

- You will see more disciplinary actions against your members.

- You will see problems that didn't exist before.

- You will find yourself with a bad reputation.

- You will decrease morale throughout the organization.

All of these bring on feelings of regret. A leader's job is to identify examples of unacceptable customer service. We spend a lot of time teaching people what to do. We should also take time to educate members of the organization on what not to do. Below are some examples of unacceptable customer service by fire service professionals:

- Failure to provide the service you promised.
  Example: This covers everything from missing scheduled appointments to failing to save someone after promising a family member you were going to do so. One of the worse scenarios you can find yourself in is trying to console a hysterical family member who is yelling, "You said you were going to save him!"

- Unpleasant surprises.
  Example: Don't create bigger problems than the ones you came to fix. Imagine arriving to a residential alarm activation that turned out to be a simple smoke detector that needed a new battery. How would the customer feel if you prematurely forced entry, left the busted door open, let their pets run out of the house, and tracked dirt all over their newly cleaned carpets?

- Unrealistic customer expectations.
  Example: What people see in the movies is much different from what they are going to get in real life. We can't scale buildings without a ladder and run through fire to rescue a Barbie doll. When confronted with people who have unrealistic

expectations, we need to take a moment (now or later) to educate them.

- Delayed responses (fig. 4–12).
  Example: Perception of time slows down when people are in the midst of a crisis. Seconds feel like minutes and minutes feel like hours. This is sometimes compounded by ineffective dispatching systems that prevent us (the fire department) from receiving the call earlier. Be prepared to answer questions like, "What took you so long?" Unfortunately, people rarely say this to our faces—they typically tell it to the reporter on the street.

- Ignoring and/or minimizing the customer's problem or concerns.
  Example: Every customer's problem is a big problem in their eyes. Don't compare incidents. A child losing her teddy bear can be just as traumatic as a couple losing their dog. Be empathetic and don't ever minimize the customer's feelings and concerns because you think he or she is overreacting.

- Bad manners.
  Example: Inappropriate language has no place outside of the firehouse. Making comments in poor taste can easily turn a good customer away. If you wouldn't say it in front of your mother, don't say to the general public. If you really want to be a leader, don't say it at all.

There are consequences for poor customer service. Resulting from the incredibly negative press we will receive in the fire service will be political fallout, lack of support from the public, legal issues, disciplinary action, a bad reputation, a decrease in morale, regret, and problems that didn't exist before. With regard to political issues, this can be devastating for a fire department. You will have bigger problems than you bargained for if the people who vote on your budget, agree to your pay, and approve the purchasing of new equipment are against you.

Another problem that comes with unacceptable customer service is what I call *the ripple effect*. One angry customer will tell everyone he talks with about his experience with you. One angry customer can spread out like a ripple that seems to travel farther than you could have imagined and appears impossible to stop.

Fig. 4–12. Perception of time slows down when people are in the midst of a crisis. Seconds feel like minutes. Be prepared to answer questions like, "What took you so long?"

....

"Unhappy customers are a concern,

but they're also your greatest

source of learning."

....

There are different types of unhappy customers. There are those who thrive on spreading the negative by telling their negative experience with your organization to everyone they come within three feet of. There are others who demand apologies, sometimes in a public or political forum. Then there are the ones who you will never make happy, no matter what you say or do. However, it's been my experience that you can turn almost any disgruntled customer into a fan if you play your cards right.

An angry couple walked into my fire headquarters one day and demanded to see the chief. I was one door down in the training office when I overheard their conversation. The couple ran a halfway house for troubled teens who didn't have a support system at home. They said a group of firefighters from our department were walking past their house on their way to march in the St. Patrick's Day parade when one of them looked on the porch and said, "Look at those derelicts!"

The couple complained about how careless this comment was. The man stressed that these kids were working hard to get their lives on track, and being called derelicts was hurtful and unprofessional. I could hear my chief backed up against a wall when I came out to the lobby and peeked in his office to see if I could help. By this time, the man was describing what the firefighter looked like. Although I was well aware of the situation, the chief asked the couple to share their complaint with me. Instead of telling them I heard everything, I let the man vent. It was obvious to me that he needed to get this off his chest, and I wanted him to have the opportunity to feel that he was being heard and taken seriously by multiple members of our department.

During the conversation, I stressed the fact that there were several departments participating in the parade and there was a possibility that it was not one of our members. The man said he was 100% certain that the person was from our organization. In fact, moments later he pointed to a photo of a group of our members on the wall and said, "That's him!" He also said, "And he was wearing a whistle around his neck." Since the person in the photo was also the band leader, it sounded like he was on point.

My chief assured the couple this would be handled internally and the firefighter would be questioned and held accountable for his actions, but this didn't seem to be enough. "What about the children?" the man said. "What am I supposed to say to them?"

I looked at my chief and said, "With your approval Chief, I'd like to go speak with them." He looked at the couple to see if it was okay with them. I elaborated, "I'm sure we can turn this into a positive. I'll talk about how they felt when the comment was made and stress why people shouldn't say hurtful things. I'll apologize on behalf of our department, and I can show them some videos and equipment, like a thermal imaging camera, and demonstrate how it works." It wasn't an unusual suggestion. Firefighters are used to speaking to and educating children and adults on a number of topics (fig. 4–13).

Fig. 4–13. Firefighters are constantly educating people of all ages on topics such as fire safety and prevention.

The man's eyes actually lit up. "That would be great!" he said. "How soon can we do this?"

"I'll do it tomorrow if you like." I replied.

They loved the idea. The next day, I fulfilled my promise and spoke with the kids. They were reserved and standoffish at first, but before I left, we were all laughing and having a great time. Everyone also learned a lot, including me. I completely understood that I was representing the department I worked for and that my job was to make this group of disgruntled customers like and respect us again. I think I accomplished that goal.

As far as the firefighter goes, I am not sure what actions the chief took. I never asked. As far as I know, it still may not have been the accused firefighter who made the comment after all. It may have been one of the members of the neighboring department who was walking with him. None of that matters. The only thing that matters was that we had unhappy customers and I had an opportunity to fix things, so I did what I could by stepping up.

There will be times when you encounter unhappy customers. Perhaps it will be the type of person who thrives off confrontation, demands apologies, and likes to tell others about your flaws. If this person is loud and others are around, invite him back to an office at the fire station where you can discuss things in private. Otherwise, avoid confrontation. You would be better off if you were kind and empathetic, listened, accommodated him promptly (if possible), and utilized the *feel, felt, why* technique described earlier in this chapter.

Unhappy customers can suck the life out of an organization because of their ability to spread negativity. Unfortunately, although happy customers also tell people about their experience, they tend to do it less than angry ones, and customers who are just satisfied typically don't tell anyone. The key is to do more than expected and wow your customers. That will get them talking.

More Than Expected

When I was a newly appointed deputy chief, my job was to cover each of the four shifts when the deputies in charge of those shifts took off on vacation. One day, I was working on the group that I was going to eventually take over, because the current deputy chief had already set his retirement date and I was next in line for my own shift. Working with this group prior to this date gave me a great opportunity to see how the firefighters and officers interact with the public.

One of the calls we responded to was a broken water pipe in an unfinished basement. We were greeted by a woman in her late 70s. She told us there was water in her basement, so we went down to investigate and found the broken pipe. We stopped the leak by shutting the water, but since we couldn't isolate the broken pipe, we had to shut the water to the house. The woman said her husband would be home soon, so I told her to have him call a plumber to have it repaired as soon as possible. She told me he would take care of it when he returned home. I asked one of the guys to wrap a cloth around the broken pipe so the plumber could easily identify where the leak was. When I returned from the basement, I discovered that the engine captain was on one knee, talking to the woman, who was sitting in a chair. He was writing something down for her. Moments later, he pulled out a cell phone, called the plumber, and began explaining the situation. After the call, he again gave her his full attention and explained that he was leaving her his cell number. He said, "When the plumber arrives, if he has any questions, tell him to call me. In between now and then, if you need anything, call us and we will come back." The woman was thankful. Although the officer's actions were not an uncommon practice on our department, what struck me was the way he was talking to the woman. It was the same way I would have talked to my own grandmother, in a loving, compassionate way.

Back at the fire station, I asked him to elaborate on the conversation he had with the woman. He informed me that the woman's husband was not coming back home. As he was speaking with her, he discovered the woman's husband had recently passed away. She told me he would be coming home soon, but it was a mistake that resulted from habit or denial. I was impressed with this captain's compassion. He did more than what was expected. I later told him, in front of everyone, that's exactly what I like to see.

Great leaders stress the importance of customer service. My job as a chief officer was to try and instill that thought process into the firefighters working on my shift. My goal was to get them to buy into the concept of *wowing* the customer. Every call, whether it is a busted water pipe, a strange odor, a sparking outlet, or a twisted ankle, is a chance for us to give more than what is expected. To provide exceptional service, you have to understand that the customer is the event. Your customers have needs, emotions, and feelings. Your job, as a leader, is to listen and exceed their expectations.

....

"People will forget what you said,
people will forget what you did,
but people will never forget
how you made them feel."

—Maya Angelou

....

People remember the heroic high-angle rescue off the roof of the skyscraper and the visual of the firefighter performing CPR on a baby as he rushes out of the burning building, but these incidents are few and far between. With that in mind, it's important to remember that the little things make a big difference. Citizens will remember the firefighter bringing their laptop or their wedding album out to them as they stand helpless in street watching us bring the fire under control. They will remember when a crew slows the engine down and waves to young children as they pass by a school. They will remember a firefighter cleaning the soot off their cat before handing it back to them (figs. 4–14 and 4–15). They will voice their appreciation when firefighters wipe their feet before walking in their home. I once walked into a Hindu Community Center to investigate an activated alarm while a religious ceremony was in progress. Everyone retreated to the front lobby of the building, and I noticed no one was wearing shoes. They told us the alarm was an unintentional activation. I told the firefighters to wait in the lobby while I investigated. You couldn't imagine the look of appreciation I received when I asked if they preferred that I took my shoes off while I walked to the alarm panel. Of course, I was an inch too short to reset the system, but this simple act made the customers happy. And it made for a good laugh when we returned back to quarters.

Figs. 4–14 and 4–15. A customer will never forget those extra things you do to show that you care, like what these firefighters did when they cleaned the soot off a cat.

Respect is at the heart of great customer service. My friend PJ Norwood understands this very well. PJ is a fire service leader and a chief officer from East Haven, Connecticut, who once wrote a blog called "The Little Things." It was a beautifully written piece highlighting the fact that we are public servants first, last, and always. In his blog, he references the actions taken by a group of firefighters from Montana who were helping fight a massive forest fire in Colorado.

The fire moved quickly toward the community of Mountain Shadows in Colorado Springs. Residents quickly evacuated, and rightfully so, since the community was destroyed. One week later, families began to return to the neighborhood, only to find their homes ravaged by fire. One family, the Barkers, were surprised to discover that their home had survived. Ken Barker initially thought this was a stroke of luck, but he soon discovered it was much more. It was a battle, and the firefighters working to protect his house won. And they saved more than just the home. Sitting under a lawn decoration on their doorstep was a piece of paper. On it was a handwritten note that read, "We removed one dead chicken from your coop. We gave them food and water." It was signed, Montana Firefighters.

Mr. Barker told a local news station that he was going to frame the note. He commented that there aren't enough words to describe how much it meant to him that these firefighters all the way in Montana, with so much on their minds, took the time to do such a kind act. "It's above and beyond. It really is, I mean, I can't say enough of what all the firefighters did," Barker said.

The note those firefighters left went beyond the few simple words they wrote. It told the much bigger story of firefighters who care and who did more than expected. Mr. Barker was so moved that he told the news station he planned to write a letter to Montana's governor.

The actions of the Montana firefighters reflected well on firefighters throughout the country. This group of individuals took it upon themselves to *step up and lead!*

How to Stand Out

I'm sure by now you get it. The future of all companies and organizations lies in keeping customers happy. Leaders have to continue to think of ways to exceed expectations. They must also reward their members for doing so. The firefighters on my team know I will praise them publicly when they treat people as if they are family members. I don't believe in taking shortcuts when it comes to making the public safe and satisfied with our service.

When it comes to customer service, in order to stand out, consider the following questions that I ask at each call I respond to:

- What can I give this customer that he or she cannot get elsewhere?

- How can I make him or her feel that we went above and beyond to satisfy his or her needs?

- What can I give this customer that is totally unexpected?

If I'm having a bad day (which we all have) and/or I'm dealing with a disgruntled or difficult citizen who is trying my patience, I imagine that a video camera is on me. In today's society, everyone has access to a camera. All people have to do when they want to record something is pull out their cell phone. We used to have to be concerned only with the people who we were directly dealing with and the few who stopped to observe what was happening. Today we have to be concerned with the possibility of our actions going viral on YouTube (fig. 4–16). This simple thought will help you stay on your game. If a citizen gets out of control, you can always call law enforcement to the scene to handle the situation.

Our customer may become unhappy if we discover an illegal apartment in the basement of his house, but we obviously have to take action. Instead of being rude, which some people tend to be in this type of situation, we can ask ourselves the question: how can I make the homeowner understand I am taking action because I have his safety in mind? This is another opportunity to use *feel*, *felt*, *why*.

As firefighters, we sometimes have to do things people will disagree with or will not like. That doesn't mean we have to be rude when doing it. Remember, someone is recording your every move. That should be enough to help you maintain your posture and deal with difficult people in a calm and professional manner.

Fig. 4–16. Almost everyone today has immediate access to a camera or recording device. All anyone has to do is take a cell phone out of their pocket.

You may be thinking that this all sounds too simple, but don't ever lose sight of the fact that most people will forget what you say and do, but they will never forget how you made them feel. When you treat people (customers and coworkers) with respect, you will receive respect in return. When people respect you, you will have more influence over them. You may be the most talented, skillful, well-dressed professional in the world, but if you look down your nose at people, what good are you? People don't care how much you know, they want to know that you care about them.

As a fire chief, if I tell a firefighter to make Mr. Grimaldi happy, it's my job to show appreciation when that firefighter does the right thing, which will make that person happy in return. If I don't show my team what I want by being the example, how would they know what to do?

If I expect the members of my department to be concerned about the safety and well-being of the civilians who live in and pass through our town, what would my message be if I didn't show those firefighters that my top priority was their safety and well-being? Perhaps we should call it the customer service food chain.

If an organizational leader wants to improve the level of customer service his or her team is providing, that leader may have to begin by changing his or her own behavior. When it comes down to it, the only thing you have complete control over is your own actions. When you wake up in the morning, the only person you can manage is you. If you can't do that, how would you be able to lead? It comes back to my favorite quote: "A leader of one can one day be a leader of many, but if you can't lead one, you'll never lead any."

Be kind! That's it, in a nutshell. A leader will always be kind, even when disciplining others. Being kind does not mean you have to be soft. It comes back to compassion—which is something you should show the people you work with and your customers. This works inside and outside of the fire service. It works at all levels. It's simple . . . so simple, anyone could do it. Don't get me wrong, if someone is doing something that threatens his or her life or the lives of others, an officer has every right to be firm and direct. The fire service is not corporate America. There are times when you will have to raise your voice to make your point. It comes with the job, but this doesn't have to be the norm, as some foolishly think.

When it comes to dealing with a customer, a cooler head must always prevail. And the service must be outstanding. Some departments frown upon members who hang up smoke detectors for elderly widows. I say, do it. Some departments may say it's not in our job description to call a teenager's parents when their child is on the way to the hospital to be cared for after an auto accident. If you have the parents' information, I say do it. Some firefighters think salvage is a thankless job on the fireground. I say it's one of the most important jobs when it comes to positive interaction with our customers. If you have time and resources to set up a water chute out a window to redirect the runoff from the ceiling, I say, step up and do it.

....

"The goal as a company is to have customer service that is not just the best but legendary."

—*Sam Walton, Founder of Wal-Mart*

....

Common Sense

So many times, providing exceptional customer service simply comes down to good old common sense. Take these following scenarios, for example. Read the brief description, then think about the following questions. You don't have to be a firefighter to know the right answers to these questions. You only have to have common sense.

Scenario 1

An understaffed fire department just finished working hard at a private dwelling fire. They made a great stop given their staffing challenges. After reporting the fire under control and overhauling, three firefighters sit on the curb and drink bottles of water. One of the residents who watched the entire operation from across the street approaches them. She is visibly shaken up. The woman asks how bad the damage is. A junior firefighter responds, "Give me a break, I just sat down." The other two find the comment amusing.

1. What did the firefighters do right?

2. What did the firefighters do wrong?

3. What is the customer's perception of the fire department?

4. What outcome can be expected from the incident?

Scenario 2

A crew is exhausted from fighting two commercial fires, when the third fire call comes in. This one is a residential fire that started in the kitchen. After performing their duties to the best of their ability, the fire is extinguished. Unfortunately, there is too much damage to let the young couple who live there stay in the house overnight. They approach the firefighters and ask what their next step is. The chief gives them a copy of "After the Fire! Returning to Normal" and tells them he is going to contact the Red Cross to assist them. They ask if it's possible to get their wedding invitations from the house. "It's the only thing we absolutely need right now," the woman stresses. The chief sends in an officer and another firefighter into the structure to retrieve the invitations and bring them to the couple.

1. What did the firefighters do right?

2. What did the firefighters do wrong?

3. What is the customer's perception of the fire department?

4. What outcome can be expected from the incident?

You and I know the couple is not going to be sending the invitations out within the next 24 hours, but if retrieving them is the one simple thing that will make the woman happy, and it's safe and easy to do, it's worth taking a minute to do it.

Once again, providing exceptional customer service simply comes down to good old common sense.

Downtime

Let's face it, when people call 9-1-1, they don't really care what a firefighter is wearing as long as he or she responds quickly, solves their crisis, and treats them with respect. On the other hand, when folks encounter a group of firefighters at a community event or on the street, they expect them to be well groomed and dressed appropriately.

Firefighters must always make every effort to portray themselves as professionals from head to toe. Anything less is simply unacceptable (fig. 4–17). Start by looking professional. This means wearing a neatly pressed uniform. Invest in an iron. If your shirt or pants are the wrong size, purchase new ones. Make sure your shoes have a shine to them. It's essential that firefighters remember that the emblem on their shirts and the patch on their sleeves belong to the community they serve and that they wear them proudly.

Fig. 4–17. Firefighters must always dress appropriately and portray themselves as professionals from head to toe. Anything less is simply unacceptable.

Although firefighting is one of the most stressful and physically demanding jobs in the world, most of the time a career firefighter spends in uniform could be considered downtime. I'm talking about times when the fire station is in order, the station housework is finished, the drills are complete, and the calls are coming in few and far between. These times—downtime—present the absolute best opportunities to connect with people.

Firefighters are public servants. To truly fulfill that role, it's important to be visible as much as possible. Being visible doesn't mean just being seen. The fact is, firefighters should always be doing "something." Our customers—the taxpayers—deserve it. Your customers need to see you producing value at all times.

An organization with a lot of downtime is not very productive. There's no doubt, there will be times when not much is happening. For firefighters, being well rested and ready to respond is important, but we can stay ready and well rested and still be productive throughout the day.

If I told the firefighters in my department (a paid department) that it was okay to sit in front of the firehouse on a bench or attend a community sporting event, I'd be giving them the wrong advice. Instead of sitting in front of the firehouse, grab a tool and conduct a drill, or wash the apparatus or hose (fig. 4–18). Instead of attending a sporting event and watching a game, pull out the medical bags and set up a first aid station, or do some kind of activities for the younger children at the event (fig. 4–19) like you would when giving a tour of the fire station. By doing these things, you will have the opportunity to interact with the community and gain fans. Yes, I said fans. If people are fans of your organization, they will support you and your mission.

Fig. 4–18. A firefighter should always be active, whether it's cleaning equipment . . .

Fig. 4–19. . . . or interacting with the public.

The point is simple: when in public, always be doing "something." Don't just be visible. The key to customer service is to engage and connect with people.

Engage and Connect

It doesn't take anything more than awareness and a little effort to say hello and talk to people in stores, wave to kids as you pass by them on the fire engine or in a parade (fig. 4–20), or stop and help someone with car trouble. These are examples of how firefighters can engage and connect with their customers.

My crew once responded to a smoke condition in a large apartment complex. From the distinct odor we immediately knew it was a pot that was sitting over a flame on the stove for too long. After taking care of the situation, we were leaving the building when I noticed a young boy hysterically crying. I asked his mother what was wrong and in broken English she said, "He's upset because he wants to be a fireman. He wanted to put the fire out."

Fig. 4–20. Firefighters waving to the crowd during a parade is one small example of how we connect with our customers.

I asked the captain on the engine if he could go to the end of the cul-de-sac, turn around, turn on the lights, and stop in front of the building to let the boy sit in the apparatus. Needless to say, we made a little boy happy and gained a few fans that day. And it took hardly any effort.

Another company was out clearing snow from the hydrants after we received more than 20 inches of snowfall one day. Shoveling hydrants is a frustrating job because many times a plow operator will cover the hydrants with a mountain of tightly packed snow. Our members often have to use maps to find them. After hours of locating and clearing hydrants (and making sure not to throw snow in areas that were previously cleared by residents), our members came upon several vehicles that were stuck. Each time, they helped shovel and/or push the vehicle back onto a clear road. Simple acts like this make an organization shine.

Although firefighters should spend as much time out of quarters as possible, they must be doing something productive, otherwise they can cause resentment. Let me explain this more thoroughly. In a challenging economy, the last thing people who are struggling financially want to see is someone standing around "getting paid to do nothing." This is especially true when they are the ones paying for that person's salary, benefits, and equipment. Again, I refer to my experience with the man in the deli. He didn't see what we were doing all day, he only saw me standing in line at a deli. In his eyes, I was the policeman in line at the donut shop (no disrespect to friends in law enforcement).

Whenever you as a leader are in the public's eyes, make sure you are doing something productive. Greet your customer's with a smile. Take actions to *connect with them*. You are a servant, and servants serve. If you see an elderly man walking by on a hot summer day, offer him a bottle of water. Get involved in community events where you can perform demonstrations and educate the public on what you do. Smart leaders in the fire service know the importance of finding creative ways to educate the public, and especially children, about fire safety (fig. 4–21). Your goal is to begin to establish familiarization and trust. Get to know people's first names. Do this when things are going good and you will be grateful. Ninety-nine percent of the time, people will call us for help, but there may come a time when you need to call on them for support. Don't make the mistake of failing to connect with the people you serve.

I tell firefighters all the time not to wait until a firehouse is closing to try to gain the support of your community. There are a select group of members of all ranks within my department who have done a great job of developing a strong relationship with the public—our customers. They have done a great job of creating the culture that has come to define our organization. You can do the same for your organization.

Fig. 4–21. Leaders in the fire service know the importance of finding creative ways to educate the public, and especially children, about fire safety.

Recognition Book

Rewarding your team members when they do things right is one of the best ways to create a culture of customer service. One way to express your appreciation is by developing a book that consists of positive letters from satisfied customers and articles praising the members of your organization for their work and contributions (fig. 4–22).

Fig. 4–22. A recognition book is a great way to show your team that you appreciate their hard work and the quality service they provide.

Every organization that provides outstanding customer service will receive letters from satisfied customers. One of the best things a leader can do to instill team spirit is to post those letters somewhere everyone within the organization can see. One way to do this is to collect the letters that you have received throughout the years and place them in a book that is available for everyone to view. This book can serve several purposes:

- It shows the members of your organization that you value their efforts.

- It serves as a book of examples of what your organization considers "outstanding service."

- It can be used as a reference book to show others how much your customers appreciate you when you come upon challenging times.

- It can be passed down throughout the years to show that your organization has always focused on the right thing—service!

This type of book should also include newspaper articles that feature your organization in a positive light. In the fire service, this book can include articles and letters about rescues, promotions, awards, challenging fires they fought, and community events your members participated in throughout the years that made your organization shine.

Don't lose sight of the fact that people like (and need) to hear the words "thank you" and "great job." Don't deprive your hard-working team of this. If you fail to show appreciation when people go above and beyond, believe me, they won't do it for long.

Social Media

When a large-scale fire or other incident occurs, the incident commander will assign someone to fulfill the role of public information officer. This is an important job that requires tact and skill, because the person who speaks to the media is passing on a message from your organization to the public (fig. 4–23). However, the message that is recorded by news media channels often doesn't run on television until that channel's news hour, which could be hours after the message was relevant.

Times have changed. I was on vacation at the Jersey Shore when I received word that my town was battling a fully involved structure fire that had spread to two exposures. I found out about the fire because one of my Facebook friends mentioned it in his status update, and another friend posted a photo of the fire (fig. 4–24). That story brings up one major question and makes one serious point. The question: why the heck was I checking my Facebook status while on vacation? For those of you with an account on a popular social media site, you understand. The point: we live in a real-time news society.

Gone are the days of taking three hours to report breaking news. Since the emergence of Facebook, Twitter, and other social networks, people are receiving their news as quickly as it happens, many times from people who are actually witnessing the event as they write about it. Want to find out who won the latest MMA fight on pay-per-view even though you didn't purchase the event? Want to hear about a celebrity who just checked into rehab? One of your online friends will surely spread the word. This same phenomenon is happening in our professional lives.

Fig. 4–23. As important as it is to have a public information officer, today's organizations need to understand and take advantage of the power of social media, which gives people and organizations a platform to pass on an immediate, real-time message.

Fig. 4–24. Since the introduction of social media, news travels fast and is often inaccurate. This photo was posted by one of my friends on a popular social media website. Others commented that the fire involved three structures when, in fact, it did not.

The funny thing is, the structure fire I read about while on vacation, although bad, was confined to one structure. My Facebook friend—a meat cutter at a deli—was providing people with the wrong information (which is a common occurrence in all social media outlets). Google CEO Eric Schmidt once said that today more content is created on the Internet every 48 hours than was created from the beginning of time until 2003. Everyone with a blog, website, or social media profile is providing information to others. Most people today don't even read newspapers. Why would you want to wait until next week for people to find out the truth about what your organization is doing?

One day my crew fought a bad residential structure fire in a balloon-frame-constructed home. We spent a few hours fighting the fire. When I returned to the station, I had 16 text messages from people asking if I was okay, including several from my wife, who lives more than an hour away. It quickly became apparent to me that I was tagged in photos of the incident that someone posted on Facebook. I soon discovered that one of our members' sons had put more than 400 photos on the social media site and began tagging people he was friends with, including me (figs. 4–25 and 4–26). Under many of the photos were comments from people about what happened at the fire. Again, most of the information was wrong.

Perhaps, as leaders, we should rethink the name "social network" and rebrand it as "public relations media." Think about this, when people "like" your organization's page, they are linking themselves to your brand. They are now saying, "Yes, I want to hear about your organization's breaking news."

We can't shut down these sites; they're here to stay. But we can embrace them and use them to our advantage. How? Start a page that represents your organization!

I strongly encourage you to consult with the head of your organization before creating an official page or website. Once you get approval, the following are some tips or guidelines to help you get started.

Figs. 4–25 and 4–26. After battling a three-alarm fire, I returned to the firehouse to discover that more than 400 photos of the incident were posted on Facebook.

Tips for creating a website or social media page to communicate with your customers:

- Clearly identify your page objective. Stay away from political opinions or sensitive material, such as religious beliefs. This should be an informative page that helps you communicate directly with your customers.

- Limit the number of administrators. One to four administrators on a page is enough to keep content current and accurate. Make sure they have permission to represent your organization as information officers.

- Don't post anything that could be considered controversial. Identifying your objectives and limiting your administrators should help prevent this, but make sure that your message is strictly limited to one that is in line with the mission of your organization.

- Pass on important community news. If your organization is participating in a community event, mention it. Remember, this is your opportunity to pass on the information you want people to hear about. That includes all the information we mentioned in the recognition book: rescues, promotions, tough fires, awards, and community events in which members participated.

....

"Why ignore or resist the awesome power of social media? News today is 'real-time.' With a social media account you can control the message of your organization."

....

You may not think it's important to start a social media page, but you'd be wise to remember that your customers have one. Before the Internet, you would have to work hard to spread the word about a bad experience you had with a company. Today, all you have to do is type a few words and your entire network can read about it. A few days before I wrote this section, a good friend of mine posted the following status on his Facebook page:

> I feel it is my civic duty to point out that dealing with the staff at ***** Pools was the worst customer service experience I've had in years. Do yourself a favor and go elsewhere!

A word of caution for emergency service personnel: In the social media age, organizations like law enforcement and the fire service will continue to struggle with blurred lines between "free speech" versus "on the job." Members of both organizations have lost their jobs because they posted something that their organizations felt crossed the line. People need to know that once they take an oath, they are representing an organization with every action they take.

One of the earliest examples of this came on July 17, 2010, when a firefighter arrived on the scene of a single car accident in which a 23-year-old mother of two was found dead on arrival. The firefighter took out his phone and shot a video of the victim, complete with graphic commentary, while she was still in the vehicle. The firefighter shared the video with some of his coworkers. The following evening, one of those individuals shared it with patrons at a local bar. One of those patrons posted the video online, and it went viral. At one point, the video was posted on more than 800 websites. Predictably, the video eventually made its way to the parents of the victim. The firefighter who took the video did not break any laws, but his actions were inexcusable. He was terminated under the catchall policy of "conduct unbecoming."

To go beyond the moral and ethical questions that typically present themselves in incidents like this, there is also a question of ownership. If the firefighter were a private citizen, the video would be his property. But because he was on duty working as a firefighter who responded to the scene, he is considered an official of the fire department. Those pictures could be used as evidence in a criminal or civil case.

Since this case, there have been other incidents in which emergency service workers have placed questionable content on their blogs, social media pages, or other sites. Most were off duty and felt they were protected by the First Amendment, the right to free speech. In 2006, the Supreme Court held that public employees are not entitled to First Amendment protection for speech arising from their official duties.

Let me sum up the point by sharing this with you. If an off-duty firefighter posts something that embarrasses his or her department, that firefighter can be disciplined or even fired for "conduct unbecoming." Public servants who have found themselves in hot water have tried to argue this is a violation of their First Amendment rights, but there is no way around the argument that when a person's employment is publicly known, that person is speaking from a place of knowledge and is representing his or her organization. Instead of getting into an argument about free speech in an effort to keep your job or prevent disciplinary action, just refrain from posting anything you would not like your customers to read. If you are not 100% confident that what you are doing or saying would make you and/or your team look good in the eyes of others, don't do it.

We All Look Alike

It doesn't matter if you are the newest member of your organization or the head honcho. When dealing with customers, we all look alike. Whether you are answering the phone or responding to a distress call, you are the voice and face of your organization. Whether it's on the Internet, around the fire station, on the training ground, around your community, at a picnic, at a seminar, or at the fire scene, firefighters are always interacting with their customers. *You* are always interacting with *your* customers. Make a conscious effort to engage and connect. Then teach others in your organization to do the same. Create your organizational culture by design, rather than default.

You owe it to yourself, your team, and your customers to exceed their expectations—every time. If your organization already has a policy on customer service, follow it and build on it. If you do not have a policy, create one yourself and present it to your superiors. If they don't implement it, it doesn't mean you can't do the things outlined in this chapter (and this book). It's your obligation, as a leader, to under-promise and over-deliver. It's your decision whether or not you are going to *step up and lead!*

5

CALL TO ACTION

Problems Are Opportunities

Every adversity you and your team will ever encounter is either a problem or an opportunity. Although one might think there are many different variables that would distinguish one from the other, there is really only one difference between the two—attitude. That's right. Oftentimes the difference between a problem and an opportunity has everything to do with how you look at the challenge at hand.

Opportunities exist everywhere, but they are often disguised as challenges or problems. Of course, the opportunities may not always be so obvious, but they are always there, no matter how dire the situation appears. Problems are obstacles, but leadership is about overcoming obstacles. The level of success you and your team will achieve will be in direct proportion to your ability to adapt and overcome. Show me a championship team that has beaten the odds in any arena, and I will show you a team that has a leader who has mastered the art of overcoming.

In the fire service, we fight fires, overcome challenges, and prepare for new fires and new challenges. The fire we fought yesterday is yesterday's news because no two fires are the same. We have to prepare to fight another—different—fire tomorrow.

As a leader, your job is to prepare for success. Hope is not a strategy. You will certainly have to take calculated risks along your journey because it's the only way to put yourself in a position to achieve bigger goals. However, things can and often do go wrong at one point or another. Much of your success will be a result of your ability to solve problems. Firefighters know this better than anybody else. They exist to solve problems. When it comes to leading a team, great things often follow adversity, if you have the guts to face it head on and not use it as an excuse to fail. Every time you overcome an obstacle, you become stronger, wiser, and more capable.

....

"Problems are good, not bad.
Welcome them and become the solution."

—*Mark Victor Hansen*

....

The next time you are in a room full of your peers, look around and pick the person who has achieved the highest level of success. You will also be looking at the person who has failed the most. These people look at challenges and failure differently from most. They understand that crisis is not the developer of character. Crisis is the greatest revealer of character. They understand that once people deal with and overcome big problems, they equip themselves with confidence, ability, and the proper mind set to be able to do it again.

High-Pressure Decision Making

When problems surface, it will be easy to try to take a poll to see what everyone thinks, but too many unnecessary opinions will often lead to stagnation. Certainly, you want your team involved in the decision-making process, but when hard decisions must be made (such as those to be made on the fireground), you have to be willing to make and act on them.

The best way to overcome adversity is to face it head on. You can only do this by stepping out of your comfort zone, which means that you will have to learn how to get comfortable being uncomfortable. This may sound like lip service, but I spent my entire life stepping out of my comfort zone. Whether it was in the fire service, in sales, or as an author or speaker, whenever I wanted to bring myself or my team to the next level, it started with the realization that I was going to have to stretch myself and take a walk on unfamiliar ground.

Being uncomfortable is not an unfamiliar place for an officer in the fire service. As a fire chief, I often find myself in positions where I have to make critical decisions under high-stress and high-consequence conditions, then set a plan in motion (fig. 5–1). There are five components to making high-pressure decisions:

1. **Situational awareness.** Utilizing whatever resources you have available, gather all the data and facts you can. Make an honest assessment of the situation you are facing.

2. **Set a goal.** You must clearly define what you want to achieve. It's tough to hit a target when you don't know what you are aiming at.

3. **Risk versus reward.** Weigh the pros and cons. Draw from your tactical knowledge, which comes from past experiences and training.

4. **Input from others.** Five brains and five sets of eyes and ears are better than one. Utilize the talents, skills, and abilities of the critical few you surround yourself with, but remember that you are in charge.

5. **Take action.** Decipher the information, develop your action plan, make your decision, and put your plan into action. When it's time to make the tough decisions, a leader will exhibit confidence and control.

Fig. 5–1. Leaders on the fireground often have to make fast, critical decisions under highly stressful conditions, then set their plan in motion.

When problem solving, you will find your job to be much easier if you have previously aligned yourself with the people (and equipment) you need to achieve your overall goals. Leaders know that a group of like-minded people is stronger than an army of one. They understand the importance of working hard to cultivate relationships with other leaders.

....

"Again and again, the impossible problem

is solved when we see that the problem

is only a tough decision waiting to be made."

—Robert H. Schuller

....

The Critical Few versus the Insignificant Many

I once heard a colleague say that change would be easy if it weren't so hard. We can take that statement one step further and say that leadership would be easy if it weren't for stubborn people. It may be true that most people don't like change, but it's also true that for every ten people on your team, there will generally be one who has the ability to influence the other nine. So one of the keys to change is to recruit your top influential team members and utilize their strengths.

I don't like to refer to anyone as insignificant. I use the term to illustrate the point that you don't want to spend your valuable time working with the wrong people. Instead, look to surround yourself with people who are mature team players. The following are six signs for determining personal maturity. Such people are:

1. Thankful for what they have and for the opportunity to be part of a team that is focused and driven;

2. Humble, with a willingness to serve others and put the needs of the customers and the mission of the team ahead of their own;

3. Edifying, knowing how to encourage and build up others; Edifiers have surrendered the need to always be right;

4. Patient, understanding the concept of delayed gratification: work hard now, get rewarded later;

5. Skillful as professionals who know how to do their job and aren't afraid to act;

6. Well-developed in people skills. They know how to deal with difficult people without taking things personally.

When you find mature people who believe in your vision, keep them close to you. They will surely become part of your *critical few*.

Once you identify those people, surround yourself with them, give them meaningful tasks, get their input, and support them. It is critical that leaders take care of the people they surround themselves with. They need to rely on you. They need to know you have their backs, and you need to know they have yours when things get tough. This is what the brotherhood of the fire service is all about (fig. 5–2).

Fig. 5–2. The brotherhood in the fire service is about relying on each other when things get tough.

Although you should identify your key players, this isn't to say that there will not be times when you want everyone's input on tough decisions. One of the best examples I ever witnessed of a leader's ability to get people involved was when I attended a meeting held by my friend Deputy Chief Mike Terpak on the topic of high-rises under construction.

My department was invited to a class in our neighboring community of Jersey City that Chief Terpak had organized. As usual, Terpak delivered a great class with tons of information on battling fires in these structures. He had experience in the area: Jersey City was ranked 13th in the country in high-rises under construction per square feet. Additionally, Terpak was in command when a small fire broke out on the 17th story of one of these structures (fig. 5–3).

The fire didn't seem like much, because there appeared to be limited combustibles and no wind to fuel the fire. At least, that's what it appeared to be on the street level, until one firefighter noticed a stiff flag on the crane that was on top of the structure. The only thing that would cause this effect was high winds, in this case, 20 mph winds— on the 17th floor. The fire grew rapidly. Terpak and his crew immediately realized this fire was completely different from the ones they were used to battling in finished high-rises. The standpipe system was not completed, so they couldn't transport water easily. The stairs were not installed yet. Fire protective coating was not applied to the structural components, and tons of debris (heavy construction supplies) was flying off the building.

The class, as informative as it was, turned out to be more than a class. It was Chief Terpak's way of inviting everyone on the JCFD, as well as local departments like mine, to participate in crafting a new standard operating procedure on what he considered the most dangerous scenarios in his community (fig. 5–4).

There were about 30 people in each class, and this was the sixth class Chief Terpak had organized. He said he was going to run about six more to ensure that everyone in his department and surrounding departments had a chance to get involved.

"I want to hear everyone's thoughts. This is our biggest enemy. We need all our best minds on it." Terpak said referring to the many talented firefighters within our organizations. "E-mail me, let me know if you want to be involved in writing a section, training to work out kinks, teaching the practical, or whatever other areas you feel you can contribute to. Don't send me an e-mail telling me a portion of our current SOP stinks. Tell me how you think we can make it better. I am asking for everyone's participation; if you don't participate, then you have no say."

Terpak understood the value of getting others involved. He also willingly admitted when a project was too big for him to take on alone. He knew he had masons, steel workers, contractors, and talented firefighters on his department. Why use only his knowledge, skills, and experience when he could get the input from hundreds of others? All he had to do was ask and accept that input.

It takes a strong leader to do what he did that day: teach everything he has learned on the topic, then ask his students to help fill in the gaps. He offered everyone the opportunity to step up. After six classes, he told me he had received 30 e-mails.

Figs. 5–3 and 5–4. This fire in a high-rise under construction prompted Chief Terpak to analyze firefighting techniques in these structures by seeking input from others.

The Dominant Thought

The skills and traits you have learned in this book will provide you with a great foundation, but it's your dominant thought that will ultimately determine how strong a leader you will become. Very simply, your dominant thought is what you think about the most. And what you think about the most is usually the very thing you attract in your life. This is why it's so important to have a clear vision in your mind of what you want to accomplish. The best way I can illustrate what I'm talking about is by asking you one simple question: what is your dominant thought?

Take a moment to really think about this before you answer. If your dominant thought all day has been to eat sushi for dinner, then your mind has periodically shifted from whatever you have been doing to contemplate the question, "Where can I get sushi?" When you focus on a goal, your mind begins to focus on solving problems in order to help you achieve it. I wanted to be a deputy chief so badly that I spent every spare moment I had preparing for the exam and the position. I was a deputy chief in my mind long before I was promoted (fig. 5–5).

Fig. 5–5. This photo of my father, brother, and me at my deputy chief promotional ceremony represents the fruition of my career goal dominant thought. What is your dominant thought?

If your dominant thought is to become a leader (or enhance your leadership ability), then I believe you will accomplish that goal. If, on the other hand, you'd like to be a leader at some point in your life, if things work out for you . . . well, move over, before you get knocked over by the people who are going to pass you.

As simple as this is, people don't always understand this point, but make no mistake about it, what you focus on, you get. We are the sum total of all our thoughts. Our dominant thoughts create the life we have lived up to this point and will create our futures as well. When we focus on the end results, we are able to set proper goals that will help us reach a destination.

Setting Goals

Throughout this book I have mentioned goals, but it would be a mistake to end without stressing the importance of setting goals.

Every leader needs to know how to set and achieve goals. When you think about it, the profound difference between one person and another is the goals that each of them chooses to pursue. If you mistakenly think that goal setting is overrated, I want to encourage you to change your thinking. Goals, both formal and informal, should exist at all levels of an organization. At the highest level, having long-range goals is often referred to as having *vision*.

The most obvious reason that goal setting is important is that it helps you identify the end result you desire. If you cannot put your finger firmly on the pulse of what you are trying to accomplish, you will find it easy to be sidetracked (fig. 5–6). So many people make the mistake of thinking they have to have it "all figured out" before they take action. Of course, knowledge is power . . . but only if it's applied. After studying team building, building successful teams both in and out of the fire service, and working with teams in various arenas, I have come to realize that it's more important for a team, or an individual for that matter, to know the *why* (what he or she wants to accomplish) than to focus on the *how* (the work needed to be done in order to accomplish that goal). The *why* fuels the team. Asking a team to work without a clearly defined end result will only lead to confusion, frustration, and stagnation. The moment the team comes across an obstacle is the moment members contemplate throwing in the towel. On the other hand, if your *why* is defined, and if it is strong enough to motivate a team, those same challenges will shrink in size and ultimately will not matter.

On the fireground, we have three constant goals. They are to protect life, stabilize the incident, and conserve property. Every task we do at the fire scene is executed with those goals in mind. We must prepare months and years in advance so that we are ready to make split-second decisions when it matters most. However, that is just one aspect of our job. Setting goals and objectives at the fire scene is different from setting them in other areas. Every time we seek to take on a new project, such as writing a grant proposal, developing a new public education program, or enhancing our response capabilities, a leader must begin by taking the time to identify and establish the proper goals.

Fig. 5–6. A team needs a clearly defined mission to ensure success. If your end goal is in focus, your environment is less likely to distract you and blur your vision.

Take "enhance our response capabilities" as an example. When my department became aware of the lack of technical rescue (TR) teams in our area, we decided to take it upon ourselves to develop one. This team would require money for equipment, specialized training, and members to volunteer to be on the team. We had to identify the reasons we needed a TR team, determine which equipment and level of training was necessary, get others to buy into the concept, and research grant programs to find a funding source. It took the better part of a year, but we accomplished the goal of developing a TR team, something we could not have done without setting detailed goals and following through on them.

All winning teams are goal-oriented. A strong leader will realize this and place the proper emphasis on the importance of goal setting.

"Asking a team to work without a clearly defined end result will only lead to confusion, frustration, and stagnation."

Goals versus Dreams

Goals and dreams may seem as if they are the same thing, but they are not. A dream is something you want to accomplish, your final destination. Goals are what get you there. Both are important, because you can't reach a destination you haven't decided upon. Dreams provide fuel. Without fuel in your vehicle, it will not run. The same could be said about a leader without a dream.

To illustrate the power of a dream, imagine a dog playing in the park, and a rabbit runs by. He becomes excited and starts to chase it. The other dogs in the park heard the first dog barking and notice that it was running with conviction. Although they can see the dog, they do not see the rabbit. This, however, does stop them from joining in on the chase. After a few minutes, the followers become tired and quit running, while the original dog continues to run with the same fiery conviction it started the chase with. Why? Because that dog had seen the rabbit and the others had not.

That story is a simple example of why it is important to keep your dream in front of you. When your dream is well defined, it is easier to overcome challenges because your mind is on the prize, not the price you have to pay.

Having big dreams is important, but setting and achieving goals is what makes a person or team successful. Once you set a goal, you will encounter many distractions. It's important that you remain focused on that goal. When a firefighter is crawling through sweltering heat, inching a nozzle closer to the slight red glow in the far corner of the room, that firefighter must remain focused on the goal—the fire—not the thick black smoke that is filling the space between him and that goal.

Goals are dreams with deadlines on them. Part of being a *results-oriented* team leader is the process of goal setting, because goals enable you to measure your progress. As valuable as goals are, don't allow your team to get carried away. When you put too much on your plate, this results in unnecessary stress, which could obviously work against you. To avoid this, make it a policy that you will set between two and five goals at a time. If more than five goals are attempted, efforts may become diffused and unfocused.

The Goal-Setting Strategy

For goals to be effective, they must be attainable and measurable. *Attainable* means that each individual and/or the team as a whole will be able to complete the goal within the determined time frame. In other words, the goal is realistic. If a goal is not attainable, it can make you feel like your efforts are pointless. It is better to begin by setting modest goals that are within reach. This lends to a feeling of accomplishment and spurs you on to more ambitious goals.

Measurable means that as a leader, you need to be able to see how much of the goal is completed while the team is working on the goal. For this to be possible, you must have measurable parameters. For example, if an organization sets a goal to increase productivity in a specific area by 25% over the next three months, that organization can measure its progress weekly to see if members are on target for hitting that goal.

You don't need elaborate tools to measure your daily progress (fig. 5–7). This could be done with a simple whiteboard and dry erase marker. Draw a horizontal line. Place the word *start* on the left side and name the goal you are striving to achieve on the right side. Measure your goal by placing dates and arrows in the appropriate areas. Don't forget to write down the reward to help keep you and the team focused and enthusiastic.

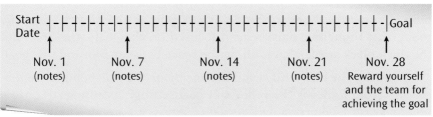

Fig. 5–7. Goals are best achieved when you use some sort of chart or mechanism to measure your progress.

If your goals are not well defined or measurable, they are nonspecific. *Nonspecific goals* cannot be readily achieved and are apt to result in frustration.

Short-, Mid-, and Long-Range Goals

Once you have formulated your goals, move them into the appropriate time frame. An organized leader will have short-range, mid-range, and long-range goals. Short-range goals are ones that can be accomplished within 30 days or fewer. These are the most common goals your team should set. They are also the most frequently set goals among leaders in the fire service, especially on the fireground where goals are set every minute (fig. 5–8). Mid-range goals will be those that you want to accomplish between 30 days up to one year. Anything after one year should go into the long-range goal category. Long-range goals are the Big Picture. Every NFL football team has the goal of winning the Super Bowl, which is the long-term goal, but the process of winning a Super Bowl begins long before the season starts. Without short-range goals, such as acquiring new talent to fill important positions or finalizing the roster during preseason, or mid-range goals, such as winning the division and making the playoffs, the team can easily get frustrated and lose focus of what is important: the victories needed to get to the Super Bowl in the first place.

Fig. 5–8. The process of setting, attaining, and reevaluating short-term goals is repeated constantly on the fireground until the incident is terminated.

The 30-day mark is an important one when it comes to goal setting. Statistics prove that 95% of people who set New Year's resolutions give up before 30 days have passed. Perhaps this is because they do not set attainable or measurable goals; however, sometimes there is another reason for this massive failure. It takes 30 days to create a habit. With attainable and measurable goals, it's easier to take action daily; after 30 days, the activities you have been doing in order to achieve your goals will become habits. Winning habits will result in greater success. It all starts with setting goals.

Ten Goal-Setting Tips

Here are ten tips to setting achievable goals.

1. **Be decisive.** The more specific and clearly you define your goals, the better equipped you and your team will be. One of the biggest, most common mistakes teams make is to lack clarity. Without clarity, you have blurry vision. If your goal is not clearly defined, it will be easy for people to be distracted and lose sight of the big picture.

2. **Stay focused.** Decisive goals that are clearly attainable and measurable will help a team stay focused, but true focus comes when everyone is in sync and all eyes are on the big picture. Work toward your short-term goals, but constantly remind your team where you are going. A focused team is less likely to be distracted and more liable to persevere through the inevitable challenges they will encounter.

3. **Put it on paper.** Unwritten goals always end up lost. There is truth to the saying "out of sight, out of mind." Many studies have been conducted showing that individuals and teams who achieve the most had a habit of putting their goals on paper. Napoleon Hill said, "Reduce your plan to writing . . . the moment you complete this, you will have definitely given concrete form to the intangible desire." When putting a goal on paper, include the following information:

   - The name of the goal
   - The deadline (or time frame) of the goal

- The priority of the goal
- How the goal will be measured

4. **Plan as a team.** Involve your team members in the planning stages. This will allow you to organize the goal and delegate tasks based on the talents, skills, and abilities of others. It will promote a sense of ownership and accountability. Utilizing the minds of others will stimulate in-depth discussions that will enable you to plan thoroughly. The more work you do on the front end of the goal-setting process, the better chance you will have at revealing obstacles early on and developing a strong game plan.

5. **Take action with specific intent.** Every action must have a purpose (fig. 5–9). Every call you make, e-mail you send, meeting you schedule, and presentation you give is done for a reason. Every time you take action, ask yourself, "Will this activity get me closer to my goal?" If the answer is *no*, don't waste your time, because you only have so much of it. Encourage your team members to think the same way, and you will be taking action with specific intent. If it becomes obvious to you that your desired goals cannot be reached, don't adjust the goals, adjust the action steps.

Fig. 5–9. After a goal is set, every action must have a purpose. Without purpose, it's easy for a team to lose focus.

6. **Be encouraging.** If you put just one bad apple in a bunch, the rest will begin to rot. The same goes with people. If the leader of the team is spreading negative thoughts or showing signs of doubt, the rest of the team members will soon follow. Be an encourager and don't allow yourself to say anything that can slow down your progress. Your team will be working hard; a high-five or pat on the back will be appreciated more than you know. Even if you encounter failure along the way, welcome it, learn from it, and build on it. It is only by confronting failures that we can come close to reaching perfection.

7. **Uphold integrity.** This means two things, team integrity and personal integrity. Team integrity: keep your team members unified, and continue to utilize their strengths. Personal integrity: make sure your goals align with your values. There is no sense in pursuing a goal that causes conflict in your heart.

8. **Suspend reality.** Don't allow yourself to filter your dreams or goals. Great accomplishments happen every day by people who refused to compromise and settle. Dream big and believe that anything is possible. If your first attempt at reaching your goal fails, review and evaluate your approach, revise it, and go again . . . and again . . . and again. Visualize your goals. See the end results being achieved in your mind. What the mind can conceive, the body can achieve.

9. **Reward your team.** People need rewards as encouragement and reminders that achieving goals is important. Choose rewards that match the level of achievement, and make sure everyone involved is recognized. Celebrate everyone's success. When you reward your team for little victories, members will get more excited about achieving bigger victories. A goal achieved is a blueprint for success; therefore, the achievement of a goal should be a "big deal." Don't forget to reward yourself and your family for the sacrifices that were made along the way.

10. **Repeat the process.** Once you accomplish a goal, you should immediately set a new goal to build off the momentum that you and your team have created. It is much harder to gain momentum than it is to lose it. Once your team reaches

its flashpoint (the point in which they are on fire and fully involved), do everything in your power to keep that fire burning!

Getting other people to commit to your vision requires communication. When communicating your message, remember the 3Cs. Effective communicators are clear, confident, and consistent.

Clear on what you are trying to accomplish.

Confident that you have an important message.

Consistent in the way you communicate and with your message.

The biggest mistake that people in leadership positions make when attempting to communicate with others is that they lack clarity. They are unsure of what they are trying to accomplish. By being unsure, they are unable to make people care about their message. If people don't care, they don't listen. Don't ever forget—confusion creates stagnation.

Balance

Although this is a book about leadership and you are reading it because you have a goal of leading in your field, I feel compelled to stress the importance of setting goals in all areas of your life. By all areas, I mean business, financial, physical, mental, lifestyle, spiritual, and especially in your family and relationships.

Jim Rohn said, "Life without balance can cost you your relationship. Life without balance can cost you your health. Life without balance can cost you your spirituality. Life without balance can cost you your wealth and your happiness. So aim high and find things to motivate you from all areas of your life. Your success depends on it."

You can wish for success in these areas all you want, but without well-thought-out goals, that's all it is . . . a wish.

....

"The greater danger for most of us
is not that our aim is too high and we miss it,
but that it is too low and we hit it."

—*Michelangelo*

....

Trust and Loyalty

You will never lead people, nor will you have a loyal team, if others do not trust you. Trust comes from being true to your word. This means you do what you say you are going to do. In the fire service, trust is the glue that holds the bond of brotherhood together. You may remember the famous scene in the movie *Backdraft*. The firefighters were battling a structure fire when the floor gave way and one of the firefighters had nearly fallen to the floor below. He was hanging on when another firefighter grabbed his arm and said, "You go . . . We go!" I was in the fire academy when that movie was released in the theaters and I still remember the feeling of chills traveling down my spine. I couldn't believe I was about to become part of a team that had this type of loyalty toward each other. The euphoria wore off pretty quickly, and reality set in once I realized that as a probie, I had to earn trust and loyalty (just as everyone else has to).

Trust and loyalty are two-way streets. Every member on the team has to offer them if they expect to receive them in return—and it's worth it, because no team can become great without them (fig. 5–10). As an aspiring leader, earning the trust of your crew is essential if you intend to develop a solid foundation for successful relationships. There are specific actions you can take that will help you to build trust. In contrast, there are also actions that break the bond of trust. Below you will find a quick list of trust breakers and trust builders.

Fig. 5–10. No team can become great without trust and loyalty.

Trust breakers

- Lying
- Breaking promises
- Spreading gossip
- Being judgmental or critical
- Taking care of your own needs at the expense of others
- Over-promising and under-delivering

Trust builders

- Always telling the truth
- Keeping your word
- Under-promising and over-delivering
- Being dependable on a consistent basis
- Not participating in negative conversations about others
- Showing others that you care about their needs

When it comes to building trust, it's all about your actions. Words are not enough. If a person says "Trust me," my immediate thought is, "You mean I couldn't trust you before?" When someone starts a sentence with, "To tell you the truth . . . " I'm thinking, "So, you've been lying to me up to now?" People with integrity don't have to tell you they are acting with integrity; their actions do the talking for them.

. . . .

"It takes a very long time to build a good house with a strong foundation and solid structure. That house can be destroyed by a fire within minutes. The same can be said about trust."

. . . .

Trust is a learned behavior

How do you get your team to trust one another? It begins when you, as a leader, show that you trust them. People will follow your lead. When you treat a valued team member with respect and dignity, others will begin to do the same. You must be the model for trust and integrity. If you are not, you run the risk developing a fickle and disloyal team. In the corporate world, this will result in failure. On the fireground, it can be disastrous.

Call to Action

Once you make the decision to lead, you'll be under pressure to reconsider your choice, to compromise, to change courses, or to give up. I say this because when you try to change the status quo, you will upset people. When you upset people, they try to stop you. It's important to recognize the fact that the world's job is to get you to lower your standards. People around you who are less ambitious will be happier if you choose the status quo over the role of a leader. But the moment you choose to lead, you'll discover that it's not so difficult.

Instead of wondering who you are upsetting, you would be better off thinking about who you are reaching. In other words, are you connecting like-minded people through your vision? That's what a leader does. A leader talks about what he or she envisions, finds others who agree that change is needed, and leads them.

As a leader, you will also take risks. Those you are leading need to see this. They need to see you being the first one to enter the danger zone and the last one to leave. They need to know you are leading by action, not by words. They need to know, without a shadow of a doubt, that you are committed to a cause.

You already know that you must exceed the expectations of your customer. Now, it's time to set expectations for yourself. This is your call to action. It's time to find something that needs to be changed, assemble a team, and change it. It's time to organize a group of people who lack direction. It's time to take charge and do the right thing. It's time to commit. It's time for you to *step up and lead!*

INDEX

program development, 148–149
standard operating procedures, 145
tips, 173
training, 168

Z

Ziglar, Zig, 124